Revolutionary Politics

Revolutionary Politics

Mehran Kamrava

PRAEGER

Westport, Connecticut
London

Library of Congress Cataloging-in-Publication Data

Kamrava, Mehran.
    Revolutionary politics / Mehran Kamrava.
        p. cm.
    Includes bibliographical references and index.
    ISBN 0-275-94444-1 (alk. paper)
    1. Revolutions.   I. Title.
    HM281.K36 1992
    303.6'4—dc20   92-23060

British Library Cataloguing in Publication Data is available.

Library of Congress Catalog Card Number: 92-23060
ISBN: 0-275-94444-1

First published in 1992

Praeger Publishers, 88 Post Road West, Westport, CT 06881
An imprint of Greenwood Publishing Group, Inc.

Printed in the United States of America

The paper used in this book complies with the
Permanent Paper Standard issued by the National
Information Standards Organization (Z39.48-1984).

10 9 8 7 6 5 4 3 2 1

Contents

Preface

This work examines the causes, processes, and outcomes of revolutions. The aim here is not to propose a new and previously unknown theoretical framework that explains revolutions in their totality. Rather, I have tried to postulate a broad, overall analytical framework within which the various facets of revolutions can be explained and examined. As a result, my focus here has been neither detailed historiography nor overt and singular reliance on one, specific theoretical approach to the study of revolutions or the broader disciplines of political science and sociology. I have, admittedly, liberally borrowed relevant concepts and approaches from various (and at times contradictory) schools of thought, intending all the while to construct a broad framework that is at the same time both theoretically consistent and yet allows for historical differences.

I would like to express my gratitude to a number of people who in various ways assisted me for this project. I am deeply grateful to John Dunn for instilling in me a deep curiosity about the causes and workings of revolutions, and, more importantly, for helping me formulate my thoughts on the subject during my studies in graduate school. I am also thankful to the students in my courses at Rhodes who were the first audience for much of this book. The greatest support and love came from my family, who, although in a different city, always acted as long distance cheerleaders and made the arduous task of writing the book much easier. Invaluable help from Michael Garret of Rhodes College

Computer Center and Praeger's Meg Fergusson greatly speeded up the final preparation of the manuscript. The book's mistakes and shortcomings are, of course, my own responsibility.

1

Introduction

This book examines the causes, processes, and consequences of revolutions. It seeks to identify elements within social and political systems that are pivotal in determining the character and nature of revolutions and revolutionary movements. First, however, certain analytical points need to be clarified. To begin with, it is most important, not just for the sake of historical accuracy but, more significantly, for the sake of analytical credibility, to differentiate between actual revolutions and the many other events that pretend to be revolutions. Which historical developments, it is important to ask, are indeed revolutions as opposed to those that are merely labeled as such for the sake of political expedience and rhetoric? The tendency of potential revolutionaries to exaggerate the historical importance of their efforts and to dramatize their "revolutionary" deeds does not help the blurred distinctions that often surround such events. More frequent is the distorted claim to revolutionary legitimacy by an incoming military junta, especially in the Middle East, where Egypt's Free Officers's "revolution" in 1952 set the stage for a host of similar revolutions in Iraq, Syria, and Libya. Often, however, the only shared characteristic that such regimes have with genuine post-revolutionary systems is the name of "revolutionary command council" or other, equally ostentatious titles with which their principal ruling groups are referred to. Some of these regimes may indeed go so far as to espouse genuinely revolutionary goals and ideals, as did in fact those governments that followed military coups in Egypt and in Ethiopia.

It is here where a multidimensional level of analysis, one which considers the *social* as well as the *political* characteristics of pre- and post-revolutionary systems, demonstrates its utility. Whereas the political dogmas and the actual policies of military-based regimes may be ostensibly revolutionary, it is their confluence with specific social and cultural characteristics in post-revolutionary societies that determines whether the outcome of the forces unleashed are indeed revolutionary or are merely symptoms of a socially vacuous military coup. Revolutions engulf not just political structures but also the cultural and social settings in which they take place. As chapter two will demonstrate, the circumstances that give rise to revolutions are not just political but are social and cultural as well, and by the same token consequences of revolutions are not limited to the political domain alone. Revolution is a product of not just turmoils and upheavals within the political establishment but also a result of social dynamics that are conducive to mass-based, revolutionary mobilization. Military coups, even of the type that ushered in the Nasserist era in Egypt, have few or no social and cultural precursors. Similarly, post-revolutionary societies acquire certain characteristics that are the unique result of revolutionary movements. The nature and characteristics of post-revolutionary societies will be elaborated on in detail in chapter four. Suffice it to say at this point that such societies embody features such as increased politicization of the broad masses, the development of a sense of collective identity, greater desires for continued mass participation, and increased demagoguery and ideological polarization, all of which are the social byproducts of revolutions. For the most part, these are not characteristics that are necessarily readily found in nations having experienced military coups. Thus, to be able to distinguish between an actual revolution and one proclaimed by actors in search of legitimacy, analysis needs to focus on the political and social *causes* and *consequences* of the events under review.

The following chapters lay out a theoretical framework according to which the causes, processes, and outcomes of revolutions can be analyzed. Chapter two examines the underlying dynamics that bring about revolutions and revolutionary movements, and the processes which revolutions undergo in their attempt to overthrow the established order. Revolutions are seen here as movements that arise from within societies and directed at capturing state power. They are spearheaded and carried forward by groups who are for one reason or another disenchanted with the political establishment. By nature, therefore, they involve the interplay of not only political dynamics that facilitate the mechanics of capturing state power, but also social and cultural dynamics within the context of which revolutionary mobilization and activity take place. Chapter three analyzes the peculiar characteristics that revolutions assume after they succeed and outlines the broad contours of post-revolutionary states. Such states, the chapter argues, are the products of intense and, in fact, often brutal attempts by former revolutionaries to give tangible, institutional meaning to their newly-won powers. Not all leaders of revolution survive the revolutionary process, many of those who weathered the repressive storms of the *ancien régime* falling at the brutal hands of their former comrades. The heirs of the revolution are far more determined to hold onto the reins of power than those they overthrew, and toward this aim they spare no repressive measures. Coercion becomes a political given, a main supporting pillar of the New Order. But so does society assume distinct features following revolutions, a development which in turn affects the relationship between the post-revolutionary state and the post-revolutionary society. The post-revolutionary polity, taken here to mean the totality of state and society together and in connection with one another, is discussed in chapter four. Chapter five, the conclusion, examines the ways in which the two phenomena of revolution and political development may be connected and, in light of the wave of revolutions in east Europe in the late 1980s, examines the reasons for their democratic, and thus comparatively unique, outcome.

Devising an analytical framework according to which revolutionary causes and outcomes can be explained is, admittedly, a risky venture. Seeking to discern specific phenomena and patterns accompanying revolutions can severely undermine the unique impact that forces such as culture and national identity can have in particular social and political settings. As with other historical events, the developments and causes that bring revolutions about need to be examined and analyzed within the specific national and historical contexts which they occur. Cultural and national nuances are indeed important in influencing the direction of historical events, revolutions included, as are indeed the role of human agency and individual initiative. The framework laid out here does not overlook such unique characteristics and, in fact, takes into account the variations that may result from specific traits not found elsewhere. The aim here is not detailed historiography or intricate sociological analysis but rather to pinpoint certain trends and developments that occur before, during, and after revolutions. Toward this goal, chapter two examines the social and political conditions that prevail prior to revolutions and the ways in which those developments in turn determine the nature and overall character of the revolutionary process.

2

Causes and Processes

The forces that lead to the appearance of revolutions and revolutionary movements are engendered in evolving political structures and in social and cultural arrangements and dynamics. More specifically, particular characteristics within pre-revolutionary states, coupled with the broad, contextual ramifications of social change and the dynamics inherent in political cultures, combine to give rise to conditions conducive to the outbreak of revolutions. However, despite the widespread prevalence of such conditions, revolutions have become decidedly rare occurrences, even in Third World countries, where the social and political prerequisites of revolutions abound. Why, it is thus important to ask, have revolutions not taken place with their supposed frequency given the existence of their social and political requisites? Moreover, exactly how and what social and political dynamics lead to revolutions and at which specific junctures? It is to these questions which the present chapter turns.

Broadly, revolutions denote rapid and fundamental changes in political arrangements and leaders, principles and orientations.[1] They entail the transformation of the very political fabric on which a government is based. Palace coups and changes in leadership and in personalities do not necessarily constitute a "revolution" in the fullest sense, despite what the coups's protagonists often like to think, although it is quite conceivable that a coup may set in motion a chain of events that could lead to the outbreak of a revolutionary situation.

Revolutions are much more fundamental developments. They turn the world of politics around, change the basic premises on which political culture is based, and transform the guidelines and the intricacies by which political conduct is governed. In this respect, revolutions are distinctively political episodes, although their precise occurrence is brought on by a coalescence of not only political but also social and cultural factors as well.[2] As past and recent experiences have demonstrated, to say that revolutions are "political struggles of great intensity"[3] and that they invariably entail considerable violence[4] has become somewhat of a truism, although the 1980s did bear witness to the budding of "negotiated revolutions" in some parts of Eastern Europe.[5] Yet by and large revolutions still remain mass-based affairs of great magnitude, brought on and carried through by the mobilization of masses of people against specific political targets. Even Hungary's largely "negotiated revolution" was precipitated and in turn fueled by the vocal protestations of mobilized Hungarians in Budapest and in other cities.[6]

It follows that any credible attempt to explain revolutions needs to consider the conditions under which mass mobilization is achieved.[7] This includes an analysis of the prevailing *social* as well as the *political* conditions that are conducive to such mass mobilization. Revolutions are *political* episodes to the extent that they denote the crumbling of an old political order and its replacement by new political objects, arrangements, and structures. Exactly *how* this collapse and the subsequent replacement are brought about are manifestations of not only political dynamics but also that of all those other factors, social and cultural, which also influence mass mobilization and political activism. Thus to see revolutions as only political events is to grasp only half of the picture. Political dynamics need to be considered in conjunction with social and cultural developments.

It is within this type of a multi-disciplinary framework that theories of revolutionary causation need to be constructed and put forth. Ancient and contemporary scholarship bears witness to ceaseless and at times highly impressive efforts to examine the root causes of revolutions and to grasp the full extent of the social and political dynamics which result in revolutionary episodes.[8] Theories of revolutionary causation and consequences abound in the social sciences literature, some of which have had far greater explanatory success than others. Nevertheless, these theoretical explicandums for the most part suffer from a number of highly significant analytical deficiencies.[9] To begin with, most existing theories ignore the inherently varied nature of revolutions and attempt to explain such diverse phenomena in one, all-embracing framework. What results are theories which in their attempt to find applicability to *all* revolutions become at best too generalized.[10] The need for specificity is both historical and contextual. Revolutions vary from one another according to the different historical contexts within which they occur.[11] Thus a theoretical framework which explains the causes of, say, the French Revolution may not necessarily apply to more contemporary examples.

Yet the necessity of historical specificity in a theory of revolutions pales in comparison to the importance of its attention to the significant role that human agency plays, which is by nature reflexive and changeable. A theory of revolution needs to consider the intrinsic changeability that is imparted to revolutions because of human initiative.[12] More than anything else, the actual success or failure of revolutions depend on the specific actions taken by revolutionary participants, actions which are inherently varied according to the context, the timing, and the manner of their execution.[13] The decisions which revolutionary leaders make, the manner in which those decisions are implemented and pursued, and the specific consequences that may arise from them differ from one case to another. It is precisely these vital details that make each revolution different. Even in cases where deliberate attempts are made to emulate previous models, as, for example, Che Guevara tried in Bolivia, the striking differences in the detailed mechanisms by which revolutions are carried forward become plainly clear. It is precisely this lack of attention to contextual specificity, at the heart of which is the variable nature of human conduct and initiative, that has led to the demise of so many emulative revolutionary movements around the world.[14]

In addition to their overly ambitious and thus highly generalized nature, most theories of revolution put too much emphasis on one aspect of revolutionary eruption at the expense of other, equally significant ones. Among the theories of revolution which in recent years have gained widespread respect and currency within the academic community, emphasis has been placed either on the "dissynchronization" of value systems and the ensuing "disequilibrium" of pre-revolutionary societies;[15] on the inability of social actors to fulfill their wants and aspirations;[16] on the regime's incapacity to absorb emerging groups into itself[17] or to mobilize them to its own benefit;[18] or on the state's inability to withstand the pressures brought on it by structural weaknesses and by class-based revolts.[19] In virtually all of these approaches, overwhelming emphasis is placed on one facet of social and/or political developments while the simultaneous contribution of other dynamics are undermined or completely ignored.[20] In a few instances, emerging developments have forced a revision of earlier, one-faceted theories.[21]

But the tendency to give primacy to one aspect of analytical examination while underestimating the importance of others still pervades current scholarship on revolutions. Within this broad analytical framework, the dynamics that result in the appearance of revolutionary circumstances are political as well as social. Politically, the outbreak of revolutions require a significant weakening of the powers of political incumbents and their growing incapacity to hold on to the state's powers and its various other resources. These include loss of control of the means of economic hegemony over the general population, discontinued control over not only the coercive organs of the state, such as the army and the police, but also over the regime's propaganda networks such as the electronic and print media, and a steady loss of privileged access to socially valued goods and institutions. In general, the primary precondition of revolution is the loss of previously-held powers and privileges on the part of the elite. This reduction in the elite's powers may be caused by any number of domestic or international developments which could adversely affect the powers of the state. Internationally, such a weakening could occur through inter-state disputes and military conflicts, or excessive diplomatic pressures or conditional relations.[22] Internally, the elite's hold on power may be weakened by such events as the demise of a central, authoritarian personality, or excessive and naked competition over power resources.

Concurrently, however, the political exigencies thus created need to be exploited by the efforts of groups who take specific acts in order to bring about the regime's collapse. Unless and until such groups exist, and acquire powers sufficient to overwhelm those of the dying regime, a revolution will not occur. In essence, revolutions are raw power struggles of the highest order: on the one hand exist the political elite, in control of the state, their powers and privileges steadily declining due to a variety of internal and/or international developments; on the other hand there are revolutionaries, increasingly belligerent and with more specific demands, gradually achieving enough size and strength to overpower and replace the elite.

These political dynamics cannot occur in a social vacuum. The growing momentum of the contenders of power, who are gradually seen as--and who come to see themselves as--revolutionaries, and the withering of the state, both take place within and, in fact are precipitated by, social and cultural dynamics. Social developments help in the structural weakening of the state in a number of ways. Most fundamentally, social change and industrial development lead to the creation of various social classes and values which the existing system cannot absorb into itself.[23] Thus, especially in modernizing societies, where new classes are continuously emerging and where old and new values are in constant flux, the state assumes an essentially conflictual relationship with emerging social groups and seeks constantly to sever their access to sources of political power. Regardless of the eventual outcome of this state-society conflict, even if society has been subdued and subjected to the state's full control, the very existence of such an adversarial nexus weakens the basic foundations of the regime and increases the likelihood of its collapse.

A more important contribution that social dynamics make to revolutionary outbreaks is in augmenting the extent of popular support enjoyed by revolutionaries among the general population. By their very attempts to communicate with the masses and to get their increasingly revolutionary message across, emerging revolutionary groups employ various social medians, some of which they may not even be aware of. The existence of a number of social and cultural factors can either significantly enhance or curtail the legitimacy of political contestants and influence their respective longevity and political viability. Depending on the specific conditions within a given society, apathy, and conservatism may drown a revolutionary group into oblivion, with its cries of injustice and calls to revolt falling on ears deafened by passivity and content. Yet at the same time, social conditions may invoke in people not only a sense of injustice and deprivation, but also nationalist and religious sentiments which make them highly amenable to revolutionary mobilization. The prevalence of specific social conditions that lead to revolutionary action, and the exact nature of the link between the existing conditions and the types of responses evoked, are context-specific and vary from society to society. What is clear is that social conditions do in fact influence revolutions, more specifically revolutionary mobilization and action, in highly significant and far-reaching ways.

In analysing the causes, the course, and the outcome of revolutions, a multi-disciplinary approach of the type laid out above finds particular applicability. Politically, revolutions often take place in systems that are not highly evolved and have not reached a particularly notable degree of institutional and organizational differentiation. Within this context, contemporary, twentieth-century revolutions invariably occur in the comparatively underdeveloped political systems of the Third World, particularly those that embody "praetorian" characteristics.[24] Even the so-called "classic" revolutions that occurred prior to the classification of the "Third World" as such-- those in France and in Russia, to name two examples--evolved in political atmospheres that are not unlike the ones existing in today's pre-revolutionary, praetorian, Third World polities. In praetorian systems, social and political forces confront each other nakedly, in their most brute form, seeking aggressively to implant themselves and to supplant others. This polarization is further accentuated by the fragility of norms that govern political conduct, underwrite social relationships, and support existing institutions.[25] Within this context, while the state-society links are more tenuous, their relationship with each other is a much more consequential one. In the Third World particularly, changes occurring in the state can far more dramatically affect society than is the case in the West. Adversely, changes taking place in Third World societies can have far more dramatic political ramifications than they would in Western countries. Examining revolutions thus requires detailed analysis of political dynamics that lead to the state's weakness and to the emergence of its avowedly revolutionary foes, in addition to the development of social and cultural conditions conducive to popular revolutionary mobilization. State breakdown is only one facet of revolution. The social and cultural milieu within which it occurs is just as important.

STATE BREAKDOWN

Revolutions are brought about through a confluence of political developments and social dynamics which weaken the powers of governing incumbents and at the same time augment the capabilities of those aspiring to replace them. The political dynamics at work involve the incumbents's loss of legitimacy, the growing weakness and vulnerability of the structures and the organizations they have at their disposal, and the concurrent activities of revolutionary groups aimed at exploiting these emerging exigencies and the resulting mobilization of masses toward revolutionary goals. Equally significant are the prevailing social and cultural conditions that are conducive to revolutionary mobilization, be they a general sense of deprivation among various social strata or disenchantment over emerging social values. Also important are the means of access which revolutionary groups have to the general population, determined in turn by either existing social organizations or by alternative nexes that are specifically forged for this purpose.

It is only through a concurrent appearance of all of these dynamics, from legitimacy crisis and structural breakdown to revolutionary activism and socially and politically conduced mass mobilization, that a political revolution in the fullest sense takes place. Otherwise, in instances where emerging political weaknesses and vulnerabilities are not exploited by revolutionary groups, or when self-proclaimed revolutionaries operate in a social vacuum and seek to overthrow a strong and viable state, what occurs is merely political instability and upheaval but not revolution. It is important also to distinguish between a revolution and a palace coup, the latter resulting merely in a change of personalities while the former denotes an all-encompassing change in political arrangements, institutions,

and practices. Coup leaders all too often proclaim themselves
revolutionaries and declare their reign to be the start of a
revolutionary era. It was indeed a military coup that brought
the Ethiopian revolution to a head and dawned the post-Haile
Sellassie era.[26] However, the Ethiopian example has not been
widely repeated, and the vast majority of military coups,
especially in Latin America and Africa, result in a change of
political personalities rather than principles. Politicians are
only actors in the political drama. Their replacement with other
actors does not necessarily affect the outcome of the play. It is
the institutions which they create and which they in turn occupy,
and the ideologies and principles which they espouse, that
constitute the political drama itself and affect society at large.
Revolutions involve changing not only political actors but the
entire scenario on which the drama of politics is based.

With this in mind, it is important to remember that the key
to all successful revolutions, the catalyst that sets into motion all
of the other dynamics which produce revolutionary
circumstances, is the political incapacitation of the ruling elite.
Revolutions are in the first order developments that result from
the political crises that engulf those in power. This centrality of
state power arises out of the state's control over the various
prized resources in society. Especially in the Third World, the
state not only has power over the army, the police, and the
bureaucracy, it also controls, directly or indirectly, various
aspects of economic life, including resources, services, and general
economic activity. In short, the state controls most if not all of the
essential tools and resources that are necessary for the running of
the country. Unless and until this control is somehow weakened
and is in turn transferred over to centers outside of the state, then
aspiring revolutionaries will not find sufficient resources with
which to mount and to maintain a political takeover.

The political weakening of pre-revolutionary states can be
caused by the appearance of three broad categories of
developments. Most directly consequential in bringing about
revolutionary situations, and by far the most common set of
developments weakening state power, are those with direct
negative bearings on the state's cohesion and organizational
viability. These are developments which lead directly to the
structural collapse of state organizations and institutions.

Developments as diverse as wars, economic bankruptcy, or the death of a central figure in a personalized system, are among those category of events which can dramatically reduce the state's continued ability to control the resources needed to stay in power. Similar consequences may arise from partial and incomplete processes of political modernization, thus leading to overstretched bureaucracies incapable of dealing with evolving circumstances, unfulfilled demands for increased political participation, and a general absence of society-wide political entrepreneurship. Lastly, there is the development of a situation best described as a "crisis of legitimacy," engulfing political leaders and hence reducing their ability to rule and to stay in power.

Legitimacy Crisis, Structural Collapse

These developments are not mutually exclusive and in fact often occur in connection with one another. The relationship between crises of legitimacy and structural collapse is an especially strong one. In fact, these two developments are naturally interrelated and reinforce one another. This relationship of mutual reinforcement assumes particular importance in Third World countries, where the very process of development can create crises of legitimacy for political incumbents. Questioning the legitimacy of political leaders is an inevitable ramification of the intertwined processes of industrial growth, social change, and political development. The development syndrome results in a widening of perceptions on the part of ever larger numbers of people and, therefore, an increase in sensitivities about possible alternative ways of doing things in all phases of life.[27] What occurs is a "dissynchronization" between the values that political leaders hold on the one hand and those of the general population on the other.[28] More specifically, crises of political legitimacy arise when the claims of current leaders to power are based on socially unacceptable historical or ideological interpretations, when the degree of political socialization has not been sufficient to convince the people of the legitimacy of existing political arrangements, and when there is excessive and uninstitutionalized competition for power.[29] In essence, a legitimacy crisis arises out of inadequate and incomplete political institutionalization, itself an endemic mark of Third World political systems.[30] Thus a structural analysis of the collapse of pre-revolutionary states must necessarily examine legitimacy crises that concurrently accompany them. Legitimacy crisis is basically a crisis of authority. It signifies the inability of political leaders to justify their continued hold on power.[31] As mentioned earlier, legitimacy crisis is inherent to the process of development. However, a number of specific dynamics exacerbate the withdrawal of the proverbial "mandate of heaven" and heighten a regime's sense of illegitimacy among the population at certain historical junctures. The problem is one of inability to deliver the goods promised or in demand, be they economic, political, or emotional.[32] Lack of dynamic leadership and political acumen, continued and persistent demands for greater political participation or increased economic gratification, or a neglect or abuse of sources with symbolic importance, such as religion and nationalism, can all significantly accentuate popular perceptions about a regime's illegitimate claims to power and unfitness to govern.

Structural weaknesses in turn augment the potency of legitimacy crises by compounding the difficulties faced by supposedly incompetent leaders, and by giving added purchase to people's negative feelings about the regime. Moreover, the sense of illegitimacy that prompts people to demonstrate their displeasure with political leaders has important consequences for mass mobilization, when prevailing circumstances allow. Here again, the relationship between structural variables and legitimacy crisis is crucial in pushing revolutions.

Within the plethora of social and political developments that bring to a head the eruption of legitimacy crisis, the role of political leadership is central. This centrality arises from the fact that it is the legitimacy of political leaders that is at the very heart of legitimacy crisis. This propensity toward a sense of illegitimacy in leadership is even stronger in countries subject to intense social change, where, through diffusion or imitation, the populace is constantly striving to attain political liberties prevalent elsewhere. Again, the distinct characteristics that contemporary Third World systems have make them especially susceptible to revolutionary eruptions, particularly in comparison to the political systems of the West. In varying degrees, Third World leaders need constantly to react to, or at least to justify not abiding by, the standards which underlie the Western world because their populations are inclined to criticize, albeit often implicitly, the basis of political authority based on such foreign standards.[33]

Authoritarianism and Revolution

It is no accident that revolutions have historically taken place in decidedly antidemocratic, authoritarian states.[34] Within the specific context of the Third World, exclusionary regimes, which do not bother to mobilize popular support in order to justify their narrowly-based sources of authority, are seen as particularly illegitimate and are most vulnerable to the outbreak of revolutions.[35] Such regimes are often based on the rule of a single, all-powerful political figure and have an increasingly narrow base of support.[36] The blatant corruption of the elite that is frequently endemic to these regimes, their tight control over education and the press, the control of the economy by a few families, and their frequent neglect of national interests in preference over the interests of the superpowers, all combine to significantly increase the likelihood that such polities fall victim to crises of legitimacy.[37] Nevertheless, even these brittle political systems can stave off revolutions if they acquire the patronage of a sufficiently strong segment of the population, especially the middle classes.[38]

Yet the relationship between political leaders and legitimacy crisis extends to more than the mere maintenance of popularly-acceptable political practices and interpretations. Political leaders can significantly enhance or harm their popular legitimacy depending on how they treat the various symbols which are held in high value by important social classes. Most notably, the political leaders's neglect or offensive treatment of nationalist values and sentiments, historical traditions and cherished cultural values, and religious beliefs and symbols can dramatically reduce their legitimacy. In order to bring the prevailing social and cultural principles in concert with their political doctrines and ideologies, political leaders often interpret socially pervasive symbols in a manner that would fit

their narrow purposes, regardless of how twisted or even
offensive those interpretations may be. Interpretations ascribed
to specific historical episodes and to religious values, in
particular, are used extensively in augmenting the legitimacy of
existing political institutions and practices.[39]
Manifestations of nationalism play an even bigger part in
accentuating the popular sense of illegitimacy ascribed to
political leaders in developing countries.[40] Colonial or
neocolonial relations generate the most potent sense of
nationalism and are most conducive to legitimacy crises for
colonial powers or their local proxies. Other forms of less-
dependent relationships are also instrumental in bringing into
question the legitimacy of existing elites by heightening a
perception of their subservience to foreign powers.[41] Yet the
linkage between legitimacy crisis and nationalism is more than
one of political sensitivity. Nationalist sentiments can be
offended through the appearance of economic and industrial
subservience to a foreign country. A group of elites may
effectively cultivate a sense of political nationalism and in fact
exploit it to their benefit. However, the economic policies that
they pursue, especially if their strategy of economic development
is one of import-industrialization substitution,[42] can give rise to
sentiments of economic nationalism and discredit their
legitimacy as genuinely national leaders. Similarly, intense
propagation of Western values and norms by governing elites and
ensuing backlashes among social classes can have similar effects.

The Economic Roots of Revolution

In addition to demands for greater political participation
and the upholding of values with symbolic importance, crises of
legitimacy can arise out of a government's inability to meet
evolving economic demands and expectations. The inability to
"deliver the goods," politically and emotionally, represent only
two of the shortcomings that lead to legitimacy crisis. A
government's inability to deliver more tangible goods, those
which directly affect the economic well-being of the population,
can have even more direct bearing on its perception as legitimate
or illegitimate. Similar to antidemocratic, authoritarian states,
those countries that are in a comparatively disadvantageous

economic position are more prone to revolutions.[43] Not unlike growing demands for greater political participation, often arising out of diffusion of or exposure to Western political practices, the transitional nature of economic development breeds rising expectations, thus accentuating the legitimacy crisis of those regimes unable to meet such expectations.[44] In instances where "there is the continued, unimpeded opportunity to satisfy new needs, new hopes, new expectations," the legitimacy of political leaders is greatly enhanced and the probability of a revolutionary outbreak is reduced to a minimum.[45] When there is widespread economic deprivation, however, whether actual or perceived, real or relative, the likelihood of opposition to a regime is significantly increased, especially when that regime is seen as an obstacle to continued economic mobility.[46]

Lastly, the sources and the means through which a sense of the illegitimacy of political leaders is instilled and popularized among the people is important. A general feeling of unacceptability regarding the political and ideological justifications of political incumbents may already exist among a population. But how are these negative sentiments given sufficient potency and direction to be usefully channelled into revolutionary agitation? The issue is not merely one of overt revolutionary mobilization. Before large-scale mass mobilization toward avowedly revolutionary goals can be achieved, and even before the social and cultural conditions conducive to mass mobilization can appear in a society, there must be voices of dissent, no matter how faint and silent, bringing to light the illegitimate premises on which the current leaders's rule is based.

Legitimacy crisis is based on the perception that current political values and practices are not legitimate whereas some other alternatives are. It is more than coincidental that almost all legitimacy crises that proceed revolutions occur along with a general "intellectual rebelliousness," a "foment of ideas" which sharply criticize the status quo and propose ideological and valuative alternatives. The proliferation of intellectual activities that occurred before the revolutions in France,[47] Russia,[48] Cuba,[49] Iran,[50] and Hungary,[51] to mention a few, all had the affect of heightening popular perceptions of illegitimacy attributed to incumbent regimes. All too often, these sudden outbursts of intellectual activism are scattered, unorganized, and uncoordinated, without a coherent doctrine or theoretical framework emerging until sometime later. In France, for example, there was little agreement before 1789 among the many *philosophes* and *physiocrats* who were theorizing about various political concepts.[52] Russia's pre-revolutionary "foment of ideas" in the 1910s was expressed mostly through a highly amorphous literary movement. In Cuba what occurred was not a coordinated attempt to formulate a new theory but essentially "a guerrilla war of concepts, objectives, and abstractions."[53] And in Iran the evolution of "political Islam" as an alternative frame of ideological reference was only piecemeal and gradual.[54] Yet the cumulative effects of these alternative values and conceptual frameworks in undermining the legitimacy of political incumbents is undeniable.

Precisely why the flourishing of intellectual activity, which is part of the process of legitimacy crisis, occurs before revolutions is related to both social and to political dynamics. On the one hand, the characteristics that are inherent in the political cultures of praetorian systems, coupled with the intense processes of social change that they undergo, breed an environment which is conducive to the appearance of intellectuals propagating comparatively revolutionary ideas and concepts. In societies where merely speaking one's mind or even satirical writings are considered "revolutionary," any meaningful steps toward commentary and analytical writing can have a magnified social and political affect. At the same time, on the other hand, the structural weaknesses that engulf pre-revolutionary states add a special significance to the works of intellectuals and other men of letter. Even if purely artistic in value, works done by intellectuals in such an atmosphere add to the overall sense of skepticism regarding the legitimacy of the current order in general and that of the political establishment in specific.

The growing sense of unease with the legitimacy of the body politic is further compounded by the structural breakdown of the political system itself. A group of politicians who are unable to deliver the political, social, and emotional goods that are in demand are considered as being even less justified in their rule when the very organizations through which they govern start to break apart. Again, the contextual relationship between legitimacy crises and structural weaknesses assumes crucial importance. Revolutions, as mentioned earlier, are in large part a product of the breakup of the political establishment. Only after the state has already lost a substantial part of its coercive abilities due to various debilitating developments, such as military defeats or bureaucratic collapse, have revolutionary groups found an opportunity to carry forward their agendas and to gain widespread popular support.[55] Reinforcing and in fact expediting this breakup is the popular perception of political elites as unfit to rule and unjust in holding onto the reins of power.

In analyzing the structural breakup of pre-revolutionary regimes, equal attention needs to be paid to international as to domestic factors. With the growing complexity of evolving national agendas and international circumstances, economic and even political interdependence between modern nation-states has become an inseparable part of contemporary comparative politics. "Every modern state," John Dunn writes, "if it is to be understood accurately, must be seen just as fundamentally as a unit in an international system of other states as it must as a key factor in the production of social and economic power within its own territorial purlieus."[56] Consequently, the types of developments and relations one needs to analyze within pre-revolutionary states are not merely those between the pre-revolutionary state and society but also those between the state itself and other states.[57] Specifically, it is important to see what negative ramifications arise from a state's inability to meet the challenges of evolving international circumstances as, for example, the French, Russian, Chinese, Iranian, and more recently, the governments of Eastern European countries experienced.[58]

A variety of domestic developments have the potential of causing the paralysis of pre-revolutionary states and subsequently expediting the appearance of revolutionary movements. Such developments occur fundamentally within the purview of the state's organizations and its structures. Specifically, in relation to Third World or other praetorian systems, the breakdown of state structures assumes particular importance due to the peculiar manner in which an overwhelming majority of such structures have evolved. Third World countries are inundated with states that have variously been labelled as praetorian, "neo-patrimonial," or "Sultanistic."[59] For reasons discussed below, the structures supporting these states are particularly brittle and unreformable and are thus prone to being subsumed by revolutionary movements. Such regimes are inherently weak, for they cannot substantially penetrate their respective societies regardless of their cumbrous bureaucracies, or the fear and awe they instill in their populations through their armies and secret police. The fragile and often compulsory bonds that link the state to society are easily broken when the very seams that hold the state together begin to disintegrate, and the social energy released through this breakage often has devastating revolutionary consequences. It is not widespread poverty and misery but rather this endemic fragility of state institutions, and in turn their inability to control and to penetrate civil society, that is the most prevalent cause of revolutions.[60]

Praetorian systems are particularly susceptible to revolutions because they tend to breed an atmosphere that politicizes grievances that are otherwise nonpolitical. Those who are excluded from the political process and are not recipients of its patronage are especially likely to blame the political system for shortcomings that may or may not be politically related, such as economic difficulties or sudden social and cultural changes that cause widespread disillusionment and resentment. Particularly in closed, authoritarian systems, political leaders are seen as the primary protectors of the social and economic good, the all-embracing force from whom all power emanates. Eager to ascribe to themselves all benefits accrued through their rule, they are similarly blamed through popular eyes for discomforts that may not necessarily be of their doing. Precisely because of this overwhelming role played in all affairs of the country, or at least due to popular perceptions of such predominance, these elites represent highly visible and resented symbols of authority, targets that are not only easily identifiable but also serve to unify protestors with different grievances and from diverse backgrounds.[61] Also important is the tendency of such regimes to valorize political opposition and, by virtue of their repressive characters, to turn even moderate opposition into radical revolutionism.

Unlike personalized political systems, military

dictatorships and bureaucratic authoritarian regimes are not as readily susceptible to revolutions, although they are inherently just as unstable politically. The accentuated instability of personalized systems as opposed to bureaucratic or military dictatorships arises out of both structural characteristics as well as the functional attributes of the different systems. Structurally, the varying roles of the armed forces and the police in different systems are central to the extent of their political survivability. In all three types of political systems, repressive organs such as the military and the police play a pervasive part in maintaining the status quo. In fact, coercive organizations in such systems tend to be the most sophisticated and organizationally viable of the institutions.[62] Nevertheless, in military dictatorships and in authoritarian bureaucracies, the police and the army are often more capable of supporting the political order in times of crisis and turmoil than they are in personalized systems. This discrepancy in the effectiveness of coercive organizations in maintaining the status quo arises out of the different structural relationships that they have with the various governing bodies. In bureaucratic and military dictatorships, the army and the police are often the very organizations that occupy the seat of power and themselves form the governing elite. Even if not directly part of the establishment themselves, the relationship between these organizations and the ruling elite is at a much more intimate level than is the case in personalized systems. There is thus a lot more at stake for them in ensuring the survival of the political order than it might be in different circumstances.

Moreover, dictators in personalized systems often govern through creating and then manipulating cleavages between various organizations, even within various factions of the army, and are highly dependent on the loyalties they forge through patronage and manipulation.[63] They are thus constantly on guard against possible conspiracies, or at least a waning of loyalties, loyalties that frequently wear thinner as crises set in.

International Factors

Domestic developments are, nevertheless, only one category of events that bring about the structural collapse of an existing state. International factors can be as equally potent determinants of the viability of domestic structures and organizations. The prevalence of unequal economic and political relationships between Third World governments and the more powerful Western countries only compounds the sensitivities of domestic Third World political institutions to changes in the international environment. The extent of domestic structural responsiveness to international fluctuations varies according to the degree of economic and political dependence.

In overtly dependent Third World countries, several factors make the domestic power structure particularly brittle and exposed to revolutionary situations. To begin with, the over-identification of the elite with one or more foreign powers substantially increases their sense of illegitimacy in the public eye and makes it difficult for them to justify their rule on historical and nationalist grounds. More specifically, dependence on a foreign power reduces the political maneuverability of incumbent elites and circumscribes the range of their potential responses in times of crisis.[64] For the elite, the conduct of domestic politics becomes diplomatically conditional: domestic responses rely heavily on the diplomatic nuances of the more powerful state.[65] Thus incumbent regimes in Iran, in the Philippines, and in Hungary felt compelled, for one reason or another, to pursue domestic policies that were being explicitly or implicitly advocated by their stronger patrons.[66] Whether actual or perceived, these regimes felt pressured by international constraints from pursuing policies which they otherwise might have pursued in order to remain in power.

In instances of outright colonial domination, ruling colonial structures are not necessarily any less prone to revolutions as are weaker, dependent states. Similar to personalized and bureaucratic authoritarian regimes, direct colonial rule often disperses economic and political privileges to very few elite groups, often to settlers, and thus generates considerable anger and resentment especially among the middle and upper classes.[67] As if the granting of special privileges on the basis of racial characteristics, often the case in colonies, is not a sufficient precondition for widespread animosity toward the colonial establishment, nationalist sentiments and demands for political self-government further fan the flames of anti-colonial revolutions.[68] Furthermore, again similar to personalized regimes, colonial administrations are both highly visible targets for economic and political frustrations as well as unifying elements which draw together groups with diverse social, economic, and ethnic backgrounds whose unity would not have been so easily achieved otherwise.[69]

The external relations that can potentially lead to revolutions need not necessarily be of the type found between patron and client states. The outbreak of revolutionary circumstances in one country may lead to similar developments in another through imitation, instigation, or even contagion.[70] Insecure about the extent of their newly-acquired powers and paranoid about the conspiratorial designs of outside forces, revolutionary regimes often try to foment revolutions in neighboring countries in order to enhance their own legitimacy and power-base both at home and abroad. Similarly, domestic revolutionaries, for lack of indigenous role models or an ideology of their own, often idolize revolutionary heroes in other countries and try to follow their teachings and replicate their actions. Fueled by such revolutionary myths as Latin American continentalism, Arab unity, and Pan-Africanism, the "echo effect" of revolutions is amplified by the verbal inflation of what is usually no more than a handful of guerrillas.[71] Also prevalent are the contagious effects of revolution in one country on events occurring in another, a development further fueled by the unrelenting propaganda of most revolutionary states and the tendency to imitate foreign revolutionaries. As the changes in the Soviet Union in the late 1980s and their reverberations in the rest of Eastern Europe demonstrate, also important are the cumulative effects of gradual changes in world-historical contexts. These accumulated developments often give rise to "slow, secular trends in demography, technology, economics, religion, and worldly beliefs that set the stage for the rise and decline of core hegemonic orders, which in turn create opportunities for peripheral and small groups to gather situational advantage and revolt."[72]

In so far as dependent regimes are concerned, relations with a more powerful foreign patron can have either negative consequences for the viability of domestic structures or, as the case might be, a reinforcing, positive effect. For decades, for example, the overwhelming diplomatic force of the Soviet Union, backed up with military might under the Brezhnev doctrine, kept together the seams of Eastern European regimes and repeatedly suppressed emerging revolutions such as the one in Hungary in 1956 and in Czechoslovakia in 1968. In the 1960s, the Kennedy administration's policy of "Alliance for Progress" was similarly designed to contain the embryonic emergence of revolutionary circumstances on the Latin American continent.[73] This policy of containment was once again pursued with great zeal in the 1980s under the auspices of what came to be known as the "Reagan Doctrine." In speech after speech, President Reagan warned of "a mounting danger in Central America that threatens the security of the United States" and spoke of the necessity to contain it.[74] "Using Nicaragua as a base," he declared

> the Soviets and Cubans can become the dominant power in the crucial corridor between North and South America. Established there, they will be in a position to threaten the Panama Canal, interdict our vital caribbean sealanes and ultimately move against Mexico.[75]

The pursuit of a foreign policy thus shaped in turn resulted in heightened American economic, diplomatic, and even military presence throughout Latin America, from Mexico down to Grenada, El Salvador, Honduras, Panama, Colombia, Chile, Brazil, and Argentina. In one way or another, whether militarily or through economic aid, American efforts in Latin America were designed to strengthen incumbent regimes and to stem the tide of revolutions threatening the governments of the region.[76]

Incomplete Political Modernization

In addition to crises of legitimacy and to domestic and international sources of structural weakness, states can lose a substantial degree of their cohesion and organizational viability due to incomplete and partial processes of political modernization. Thorough and complete political modernization involves the progressive rationalization and secularization of authority, the growing differentiation of new political functions and specialized structures, and increased participation in the political process.[77] In almost all Third World countries, however, there has been a persistent reluctance on the part of existing centers of power to undergo growing secular rationalization and to open the system to unsolicited and undirected political participation.[78] The negative ramifications of skewed political modernization thus figure particularly prominently in Third World polities, where centralized political structures strive to pursue parallel but contradictory goals of increased consolidation and accommodative participation. Political modernization is, in fact, inherently politically destabilizing as it undermines loyalty to traditional authority, creates a need for new loyalties and identifications, and increases the public's desire for wider participation in the political process.[79]

When demands for greater participation are not met, the accentuation of unfulfilled aspirations substantially increases the likelihood of political instability.[80] The absence of any meaningful means and institutions through which political objectives and demands for participation could be channelled only aggravate the inherent fragility of the system.[81] Even those groups which gain entry into politics do so without becoming identified with established political institutions or acquiescing in existing political procedures.[82] Under repressive regimes, where political demands cannot be comprehensively formulated, much less expressed, the result is a further polarization of the inherently antagonistic relationship that exists between the state and society.[83] Moreover, partial political modernization further hampers the cohesion of the political system and impedes the growth of political entrepreneurship and national integration.[84] The political context remains hopelessly unevolved, exacerbating the rawness and nakedness with which political forces and dynamics confront each other. Such a persistent absence of "normative regulations of the means of competition," as one observer has put it, results in heightened political instability and a growing proclivity toward revolutionary eruption.[85]

In addition to structural attributes, functional characteristics are equally important in determining the longevity of various political systems. Personalized systems are comprised of highly visible, widely feared and resented, manipulative political figures whose longevity is determined by their vigilance, political will, and sheer wiliness. Patrimonialism pervades and there is a predominance of inter-elite and inter-organizational rivalries manipulated by the person of the ruler.[86] Bureaucratic and military dictatorships, along with other types of corporatist regimes,[87] are, however, more likely to extend patronage to the various social groups and try to incorporate them into to the system.[88] The vulnerability of such regimes to widespread, mass-based revolts is thus reduced, at least so long as the extension of patronage continue uninterrupted and the popular goods in demand, political and otherwise, are delivered.

REVOLUTIONARY MASS MOBILIZATION

The political dynamics that bring about revolutionary circumstances are by no means limited to the structural breakdown of pre-revolutionary states. Equally important are the deliberate efforts of avowed revolutionaries in bringing down the existing political order, as well as the situational possibilities for such groups to achieve the widespread support and mobilization of the masses. Revolutions, it must be remembered, are as much products of human initiative as they are the result of the political and structural demise of incumbent elites.[89] The existence of oppositional groups with the specific purpose of exploiting the state's evolving difficulties is an integral part of any full-blown revolution.[90] What varies from one historical example to another is the exact timing of the formation of such groups. Some revolutionaries predate the start of the regime's structural difficulties, while others begin to collect into cohesive organisations *after* the regime's atrophy has begun.[91] The crucial difference, especially insofar the starting point and the nature of revolutionary activism are concerned, is that some revolutions are *planned*, signified by the premeditated actions of revolutionaries based on previous calculations, whereas others are more *spontaneous*. Planned revolutions are typically formulated and carried out by revolutionary organizations which, due to the force of circumstances, rely on guerrilla warfare in overthrowing existing regimes. Thus the revolutions in Vietnam, China, Cuba, Algeria, and Nicaragua were all planned revolutions.[92] Spontaneous revolutions, on the other hand, acquire their leaders only after the revolutions are well underway. The revolutions in

France, Russia, Iran, and the ones sweeping across Eastern Europe in the late 1980s were all of the spontaneous variety. In all instances, nevertheless, the active initiatives of groups aiming to compound and to exploit the political difficulties of regimes is essential in bringing revolutions into fruition. Otherwise, what results are weakened states, lingering and in disarray, but unopposed and unchallenged.

Spontaneous Versus Planned Revolutions

Spontaneous and planned revolutions differ most significantly in the manner in which the revolutionary mobilization of the masses is achieved and in the role of the revolution's leadership cadre. In both types of revolutions, the paramount weakness and vulnerability of existing political institutions are necessary preconditions. In planned revolutions, however, a clear, identifiable cadre of revolutionary leaders exist who seek to expedite the regime's collapse through their activities. In the process, they hope, their stature and legitimacy with the public will increase, enabling them to augment their popular support and following. Such groups are actively revolutionary, both in name and in their goals, and seek specifically to bring about revolutionary circumstances. They in fact proclaim themselves to be revolutionaries long before actual revolutionary circumstances set in. In spontaneous revolutions, on the other hand, leaders of revolution ascend to that position gradually and only through the progression of revolutionary circumstances instead of the other way around. In planned revolutions, revolutionary leaders expedite the appearance of revolutionary situations. In spontaneous revolutions, it is through the progression of revolutionary developments that its ultimate leaders are determined.

In planned revolutions, the role and initiatives of professional revolutionaries are of highly important. These revolutionaries do not necessarily "make" revolutions by themselves, but are instrumental in mobilizing, organizing, and arming revolutionary masses.[93] Their specific purpose is to compound the structural deficiencies of the regime by turning the political frustrations of the masses into organized revolutionary action.[94] In their efforts, self-proclaimed revolutionary leaders recruit an army of their own and wage a war aimed at overwhelming the state. They have two pressing concerns: the formation of an army that would at least be comparable in strength to that of the regime; and the strategic and tactical maneuvers of this revolutionary army aimed at bringing about the regime's military defeat. It is only through a successful combination of these two tasks that a revolutionary organization can succeed in overthrowing the state.[95] For reasons discussed below, the leadership cadre of this revolutionary army is frequently draw form the ranks of the urban middle class, while the rank and file foot soldiers, the majority of the troops, are made up of rural inhabitants and peasants.

The efforts of revolutionary leaders in mobilizing and directing peasant activism require more than anything else a solid and viable organizational apparatus. In addition to an aroused and mobilizable peasantry, guerrilla revolutions require a disciplined army and a party organization that can provide the coordination and tactical vision necessary for peasant unity and ultimately for control of national power.[96] Peasant-based revolutions depend directly upon the mobilization of peasants by revolutionary organizations, making the sheer availability and effectiveness of such groups a necessary precondition of revolutionary situations.[97] Often times, spontaneous political acts by peasants has forced a scramble for the mobilization and formation of their would-be leadership.[98] The degree of interaction between peasants and the leadership, and the extent to which leaders can absorb the peasantry into their organization and to expand their power base, determine the viability and success of the revolutionary movement. Absence of firm links between revolutionary leaders and followers, especially in guerrilla revolutions where planned revolutionary initiatives play an extremely important role, can substantially reduce a movement's chances of success.[99] Moreover, for guerrilla organizations to succeed in achieving their revolutionary goals, they need to have a sustained ability to recruit new members, structurally and organizationally evolve and develop, and to endure the adversities of military confrontation with the regime.[100]

The social composition of the leadership of peasant-based revolutionary movements is often decidedly non-rural. It is, in fact, frequently the disaffected members of the middle classes, most notably urban-educated students and intellectuals, that occupy most of the leadership positions of guerrilla organizations. Disjointed processes of social, political, and economic development turn the middle classes (especially in the Third World) into inherently revolutionary groups, groups whose oppositional inclinations are likely to rise along with their level of education and social awareness. Given their greater sensitivity to their surrounding environment, the most revolutionary of groups are often middle-class intellectuals, and the most revolutionary of intellectuals are students.[101] These are dissatisfied literaty elites who have turned into professional revolutionaries. They have entrusted themselves with the task of establishing solid revolutionary coalitions and alliances which can not only overcome social, ethnic, and economic divides but which are also capable of eventually replacing the current regime.[102] In search of an audience willing to follow and to obey them, they most frequently find the peasantry.

The Peasant as Guerrilla

The preponderant role of the peasantry in guerrilla organizations arises out of a combination of rural conditions that are conducive to oppositional mobilization, as well as the political and ideological inclinations of revolutionary leaders themselves. To begin with, urban-based political activists are drawn to the peasantry by a number of practical political considerations. Frequently, a lack of political penetration by the government machinery into distant towns and villages has resulted in the alienation of the countryside from civil society. Despite detailed and large-scale control over various aspects of urban life, most praetorian governments, particularly those in the Third World, pay at best scant attention to the countryside and for the most part neglect not only the economic development of rural areas but, what is politically more important, their political mobilization or at least pacification as well. Even in instances where concerted efforts aimed at the political mobilization of rural inhabitants have been launched, large numbers of peasants continue to remain outside the influence of what often times turn out to be only halfhearted campaigns. The political vacuum thus created offers potential guerrilla leaders ample opportunity for recruitment and mobilization. In an environment of little or no official political presence of any kind, guerrilla leaders can not only recruit followers with relative ease but can also conduct revolutionary acts which, even if only symbolically important, may have a magnified effect. For guerrilla organizations, mere survival can be politically as important as it is to win battles. In the eminently political types of wars they wage, survival for the guerrillas is a victory in itself.[103]

Another reason for the attraction of revolutionary leaders to the peasantry is the supposed "ideological purity" of peasants brought on by their geographic and political distance from centers of power. Alienation from civil society also entails ideological and valuative estrangement from the political establishment. Mao, who was perhaps the most astute observer of the peasantry's revolutionary potential, went so far as to label peasants (not the Communist Party) as "the vanguards of revolution," "blank masses" uncorrupted by the bourgeois ideologies of the city.[104] Moreover, not only is the peasantry ideologically unassimilated into the political establishment, its predicaments and objective conditions often closely match the revolutionaries's ideologies. Most revolutionaries declare their aims to be the alleviation of misery and injustice, poverty and exploitation, the very conditions which in one way or another pervade most rural areas. Coupled with greater possibilities for recruitment and mobilization, ideological compatibility with objective conditions draws most leaders of planned revolutions to remote rural regions and areas. There is thus a strong connection between the revolutionaries's ideology and dogma, and circumstances prevailing in the countryside.

The development of the actual links that bond revolutionary leaders and guerrilla organizations to the mass of peasants are important in determining the extent and effectiveness of revolutionary mobilization. The establishment of such nexes and the resulting mobilization are dependent upon several variables, some indigenous to local conditions and others dependent on the characteristics of the guerrilla leaders themselves. Chief among these determining factors are the degree of the hegemony of the local ruling classes, the nature and extent of rural coalitions and alliances, and the ability of guerrilla leaders to deliver the goods and services which others cannot. In most rural regions, pre-capitalist peasant small-holders, sharecroppers, and tenants are likely to enjoy cultural and social (as well as organizational) autonomy from ruling elites, despite their tendency toward localism and traditionalism.[105] This relative, built-in resistance to elite hegemony and consequently receptivity to ideological and organisational alternatives arises out of a sense of economic security and independence, as inflated as it may be, *vis-a-vis* the more dominant rural classes such as big landlords and estate owners. The spread of capitalism and the subsequent commercialization of agrarian society is also important in bringing about peasant rebelliousness.[106] This increasing propensity toward revolutionism is not necessarily because of the increased exploitation of peasants due to the spread of capitalist relations, but, rather, is derived from a general breakdown of "prior social commitments" to kin and neighbors and thus greater flexibility and independence to act as desired.[107] Even more important, however, is the extent of direct government control over a region, or indirectly through landed proprietors acting as government proxies. Favorable political circumstances, most important of which are the existence of weak states, are crucial in determining the feasibility of revolutionary activism and possibilities for peasant mobilization.[108]

Another significant factor which determines the success of guerrilla leaders in mobilizing peasants in their support is the guerrillas's ability to deliver goods and services, both actual and perceived. People will join or abstain from opposition groups based on the rewards they receive, both individually or as a collective whole, rewards that may be emotional as well as material.[109] Specifically, in relation to rural areas, revolutionary movements have won broad support when they have been willing and able to provide state-like goods and services to their targeted constituents. The establishment of "liberated areas" secure from government attacks, the provision of services such as public education, health care, and law and order, and the initiation of economic reforms in the form of land redistribution or tax reductions are particularly effective measures in drawing peasants closer to guerrilla leaders.[110] The success of revolutionary groups in peasant mobilization becomes even more tangible when they provide local goods and services with immediate payoffs before attempting to mobilize the population for the more difficult task of overthrowing the government.[111]

The provision of goods and services may not necessarily be material. For most peasants and rural inhabitants, participation in an army-like guerrilla organization offers a way of escaping from disillusioning surroundings and finding purpose and meaning in a greater cause. Membership in an organization becomes an end in itself, a mean to fulfill desires of assertiveness and beliefs in higher goals and principles. To command and in turn to be commanded, to hold a gun in hand, and to aspire to dreams and ideals are often mechanisms through which peasant revolutionaries, especially younger ones, try to shatter their socially-perscribed, second-class image and, in their own world, attempt to "become somebody."

Social Polarization and Spontaneous Revolution

While planned revolutions frequently take the form of organized, peasant-based guerrilla attacks on specific targets, spontaneous revolutions are more elusive in their start and in their objectives, especially in their earlier stages, and tend to be centered more in urban as opposed to rural areas. Spontaneous revolutions typically begin with a drastic decline in the coercive powers of the state, followed in turn by a simplification of the political process and the subsequent growth of polarization among various segments of society.[112] Political simplification and polarization are interrelated: the growing dichotomy of society into two crude and simplified camps of political supporters and opponents polarizes the political environment and leads to the politicization of traditionally nonpolitical groups.[113] Crisis-initiating events, exacerbating responses by the regime, and the increasing weakness of the elite in the face of the revolutionaries's growing momentum all combine to bring about a revolution.[114] In this sequence of events, political mobilization takes place outside of the state's purview and in fact it occurs precisely because the state itself was unwilling or unable to sanction popular political participation. Precipitating events force the hands of those claiming the revolution's leadership mantle, prompting them to be more reactive rather than initiative in their maneuvers. These emerging leaders exploit rather than create the situational opportunities that arise as the revolution progresses.

Clearly, to minimize the role and importance of revolutionary leaders and their actions in spontaneous revolutions would result in a gross misunderstanding of the revolutionary process. The role of leaders in spontaneous revolutions increases as the course of events progress and as the revolution's features and goals become clearer. Leaders of spontaneous revolutions do in fact call the shots, but only after it becomes clear that they are indeed the ones commanding the adherence of the masses in the streets. How these leaders achieve their exalted position *vis-a-vis* the protesting masses depends on a number of developments. Most notably, they include a coalesce of their organizational and verbal skills, the cultural communicability of their revolutionary message and ideology, and their effectiveness in exploiting the opportunities presented them by the regime's collapse. Also important are the viability of the social and/or political organizations through which they establish their links with the larger society and relay their beliefs and propaganda to their ever-growing mass of followers.

It is here that the crucial role of social organizations in spontaneous revolutions becomes evident. Focus must be on the groups and classes that comprise a society's strata, the various groups that seek to overthrow the state by mobilizing popular support, and the connections that are forged or which already exist between the social classes on the one hand and the opposition groups on the other. In planned revolutions, the links between revolutionary leaders and the masses are established through the political parties that have been established for this very purpose. The ideology, structure, and initiatives of these parties are designed in a manner not only to capture political power but also to acquire popular support as a necessary starting point. In contrast, in spontaneous revolutions avowedly revolutionary organizations initially play only a marginal role and operate on fringes of the larger social and political setting. In fact, as exemplified in one historical case after another, the revolutionary organizations that evolve under the eventual leaders of spontaneous revolutions are at best highly amorphous and rather unstructured.[115] It is instead through existing social organizations that the necessary links between revolutionary leaders and the masses are established. Before having even acquired the support and sympathy of the population, the revolution's leaders are determined by virtue of their dominant position within society and by the strength of the social institutions they have at their disposal.

The Informality of Spontaneous Revolution Leadership

Whereas the success of planned revolutions greatly depend on the viability of the political parties and organizations involved, it is mostly through highly fluid, non-formal, and society-wide institutions and means of communication that the leaders of spontaneous revolutions communicate with their emerging followers and push the revolution forward. Gatherings in churches, tea-houses, community meeting places, social or ritualistic ceremonies, and other occasions in which intense interpersonal interactions at the local level are conducted can all serve as instruments through which messages and instructions can flow from revolutionary organizers to street protestors. The access various revolutionary groups have to these instruments of communication and mobilization determine which ones can call on the most followers more effectively, enabling them to eventually assume the leadership of a mounting revolutionary movement. Other factors significant in the nexus between the leaders and followers thus established include, among others, the depth and social salience of the informal and society-wide institutions involved, the sheer numerical size and popular availability of these organizations, and their degree of immunity from government reprisals. Equally important are the ideological and strategic compatibility of these social organizations with those of the opposition groups. While priests and religious activists may fully exploit the advantages of churches and other religious institutions in communicating with the masses, for instance, communist activists, most of whom reject religious aesthetics on doctrinal grounds, are likely to shun their use and thus circumscribe the scope of their mobilization efforts.

It is these differing roles of social organizations as opposed to revolutionary parties that has led to a historical paucity of spontaneous revolutions in most contemporary Third World countries. Examples of planned revolutions spearheaded by guerrilla organizations, or at least intended revolutions, inundate Third World countries, especially those in Latin America.[116] Planned revolutions occur most frequently where relatively strong (often military-based) regimes coexist side by side with bifurcated societies plagued by social, cultural, economic, and ethnic divisions. In such settings, revolutions could not possibly take place if not for the deliberate efforts of revolutionary organizations. Spontaneous revolutions, however, require strong social organizations and comparatively homogeneous societies, characteristics that are not readily found in many Third World countries. As it happens, throughout the Third World the most viable social organizations that have not been fully absorbed into the state are religious institutions, especially those with a history of political independence. It is primarily due to this reason that in non-Western countries where spontaneous revolutions have taken place, as in Iran and in Eastern European states, that religious institutions have played such vital parts in the revolutionary movement.[117] Politically independent social organisations, of which religious institutions have been prime historical examples, have afforded emerging leaders of revolutions access to the popular classes, both in terms of communication and organization, and have thence enabled them to popularize their beliefs and propagate their revolutionary actions among the population at large.

Ideology and Revolution

A final feature that separates spontaneous and planned revolutions is the role of ideology. Ideology plays a much greater role in planned revolutions than it does in spontaneous ones. By nature, planned revolutions are far more dependent on the deliberate revolutionary mobilization of the masses than are spontaneous revolutions, in which state breakdown and mass opposition activity largely occur spontaneously and with little encouragement from designated leaders. As such, ideologies form an intrinsically more important part of planned as opposed to spontaneous revolutions. Planned revolutions, brought on by the efforts of guerrilla organizations, are often guided by strict interpretations of specific ideologies. They are, in essence, as much ideological movements as they are revolutions.

Spontaneous revolutions, however, initially lack ideological specificity, especially in their embryonic stages when revolutionary leaders have not yet been fully determined. Leaders of planned revolutions know exactly what they want, that is, to wrest political power away from the ruling class, and have clear targets and objectives. In their pursuit, they develop or adopt an ideology most suited to their ends. In furthering their cause and efforts, the adoption of an ideology by guerrilla leaders is particularly important in representing an alternative frame of reference to that of the regime. Since they do not hold power, revolutionary leaders must convince their audience that what they believe in holds greater promise than what the regime has done. A revolutionary ideology is needed, therefore, to further the legitimacy of the revolutionaries and to delegitimize the views and beliefs of those in power.[118] In spontaneous revolutions, on the other hand, the ideology of the revolution becomes clear only with the emergence of its cadre of leaders. Most spontaneous revolutions are, in fact, free of any specific ideological characters until well after the ultimate winners of the revolution have become clear and have established their reign over the country. During the course of the revolution itself, differing ideologies are as much in competition with each other as are various opposition groups who find themselves at the helm of a brewing revolution. For protesting crowds, and for the emerging leaders of the revolution themselves, an ideological understanding of the revolutionary movement is summed up in dogmatic slogans promising vague ideals and rejecting the present. Specific doctrines with detailed outlines for future courses of action are conspicuously absent, at least until after one revolutionary group has completely dominated the movement. Even then, the ideological character of many post-revolutionary states become clear well after their initial establishment. Post-revolutionary ideological orientations often emerge out of strategic, diplomatic, and organizational considerations which may not necessarily be the ones that the revolutionaries originally held.[119]

Considering that spontaneous revolutions start out as non-ideological movements, the existence of precise factors and conditions that specifically facilitate mass mobilization assume particular importance. A regime's popular social base among those it governs, its ability and willingness to use coercion to quell the expression of anti-state sentiments, and the degree to which the popular classes are allied together against the governing elite all determine the extent and depth to which a population is spontaneously mobilized against a political order. A most important factor is the extent to which various social classes have been coopted into the regime and identify with it both politically and valuatively. It is precisely those groups unincorporated into the system, often unidentified and alien from it, that are most amenable to anti-state persuasions.[120] They have very little or nothing at stake in the prevailing political arrangements, and indeed frequently view them as a source of misery and grief. Given the existence of favorable social and political circumstances, such as a permissive political environment and a general willingness to revolt, these groups waste little time in showing their displeasure over the state of affairs. These expression of anti-state sentiments by one group are greatly strengthened when joined by those of other groups, enhancing the size and forcefulness of an emerging alliance united in its dislike of the prevailing polity. An alliance of the middle classes, who in the Third World are most prone to political opposition, and other, less well-placed social groups like the peasantry or the proletariat is particularly threatening to the political order.[121] Such a coalition not only enjoys the raw social and economic powers that stem from middle class participation, it also has the numerical strength and size of the lower classes, who, not having a whole lot to lose anyway, are more prone to taking risks and partaking in acts of political violence.

Non-Political Factors

Also influential in shaping the depth and the nature of anti-state mobilization are a number of otherwise politically unimportant logistical factors. Variables that in one way or another affect popular conduct, such as the weather, availability of recreational facilities, transportation routes, and opportunities for fact-to-face communication all influence the extent of mobilization and the manner in which it comes about and is conducted.[122] Expressly political factors are equally important.

The mere existence of anti-state grievances and sentiments is not sufficient for mass mobilization.[123] The political space provided by the state and by the efforts of existing or emerging revolutionaries are equally important. The extent to which the state is willing and capable of using coercion to maintain its power contributes most directly to the nature of opposition mobilization. Often, pre-revolutionary states lack the strong willpower necessary to withstand the onslaught of an evolving revolution, wavering among different options and unwilling to bear the costs of heavy-handed repression. In other instances, where expressions of opposition are met by determined responses, only sympathizers are intimidated into silence and become passively obedient. For the most part, activists are not discouraged but are rather radicalized, and the political atmosphere is more polarized than stabilized.[124]

The breadth of mass mobilization is in turn determined by the existence of specific society-wide conditions which are conducive to revolutionary developments. Several developments, not all of which are specifically political in origin and in context, arise within the larger society which make various social strata prone to revolutionary mobilization and, concurrently, have the potential of further exacerbating the regime's political difficulties. In a broad sense, these developments provide the contextual background within which the widespread mobilization of emerging revolutionaries is made feasible and takes place. More determinedly, the ramifications of these developments or at times their mere existence often serve as the main impetus for popular opposition against ruling elites, manifestations of which are made possible by permissive prevailing political circumstances. People will not revolt against a regime unless there is a compelling reason for them to do so.[125]

Political incapacitation by incumbent regimes simply provides the space and the breathing room necessary for the articulation and expression of political antagonisms. It is not, however, by itself a sufficient *cause* for the coordinated expression of anti-establishment sentiments by a reasonably large segment of the population. The specific sentiments and grievances that prompt populations into political activism *may be* political, but they may just as likely be nonpolitical, at least in genesis if not in actual form of expression. What is needed is a thorough examination and understanding of the underpinning characteristics and features, both political and otherwise, of societies in which revolutionary mobilization takes place. Then an identification can be made of those factors and dynamics which, individually or in conjunction with one another, invite an otherwise inert mass of people to demonstrate their collective displeasure when political circumstances allow.

Three specific sets of developments in any society have the potential of leading to the mobilization of large numbers of people. They are, broadly, those developments that give rise to economically-based grievances, to social and cultural grievances, and to political grievances. In their own way, each of these developments produce feelings of resentment and opposition against those who are popularly perceived as responsible for society's ills. Feelings of economic unease and grievance can potentially arise out of the many consequences of industrial development and technological modernization, such as scarcity of essential goods resulting from demographic growth, feelings of deprivation and inequality *vis-a-vis* others, and class structures conducive to antagonistic behavior. Social and cultural grievances, meanwhile, become most acutely pronounced during periods of intense social change, particularly when prevailing social values become disjointed and clash with one another. Lastly, political grievances, which are both frequent and which form an integral part of almost all revolutionary movements, arise out of such developments as alienation and desires for wider participation in the political process, nationalism, and growth of alternative ideologies.

Various facets of economic development substantially increase the potential, in one way or another, of widespread protests among the different social classes. The precise causal connections between economic development and political instability and violence are blurred and varied at best.[126] Nevertheless, under specific circumstances, development invokes certain reactions among people that can have potentially politically threatening results. On the most elementary level, industrialization expands the numerical size of some economic classes at the expense of others: rural inhabitants, most notably the peasants, find their numbers increasingly dwindling while the industrial and the middle classes often rise steadily.

Propertyless and unemployed villagers mushroom into a proletariat, and domestic migration becomes an uncontrolled, integral part of the development process.[127] Depending on specific economic policies, traditionally-based elites and upper classes are also often weakened, both politically and economically, and are replaced by newly emerging elite groups. In most Third World countries, it is thus not uncommon to find long-established landed or commercial elites and aristocratic families gradually fade into political oblivion and give way to new groups who owe their status to modern economic relations such as banking, international trade, and modern industries.

How these consequences of industrial development and economic growth on class composition affects the stability of political elites varies from one specific instant to another. Nevertheless, shifting class structures can and in fact often do influence the viability of a political system, particularly in cases where the state is dependent on and in turn patronizes a specific class. The close political and economic affinity of numerous praetorian regimes with one or more of the elite classes has frequently been one of the main sources of dissent and grievance by both the public at large and by emerging or existing revolutionary groups.

Another potential source of economic grievance that can increase the public's propensity toward revolutionary action is a feeling of economic deprivation. This syndrome is not unrelated to the development process and is, in fact, most accentuated in countries undergoing rapid economic growth and modernization. Modernization brings with it new needs, outlooks, and desires. It engenders new hopes and fosters rising expectations. Those who experience continued increase in well-being develop expectations about continued improvement.[128] "The crucial factor" in the promotion of society-wide economic grievances

> is the vague or specific fear that ground gained over a long period of time will be quickly lost. This fear does not generate if there is continued opportunity to satisfy continually emerging needs; it generates when the existing government suppresses or is blamed for suppressing such opportunity.[129]

What   occurs is a sense of economic deprivation, one that is relative to either one's past, to future aspirations, or to lesser capabilities than before but higher aspiration for the future.[130] People who feel deprived and are frustrated in their goals and aspirations have an "innate disposition to do violence to its source," which, especially in the Third World, is perceived to be the government.[131] In instances when the sources of deprivation are obscure and cannot be attributed to specific political targets, alternative doctrines and ideologies which justify violence gain increasing currency and appear as more and more plausible to ever-growing segments of population.[132]

    Also related to the general process of development and more specifically to feelings of deprivation are growing rates of inequality among various classes. Economic inequality by itself does not necessarily lead to political violence and the relationship between the two developments is context-specific.[133] In accented forms, however, inequality, whatever its causes, leads to a reduction of identification between the rulers and the ruled. In the face of continued misery and little or no identification between the body politic and the rest of society, widespread expressions of political discontent become highly likely.[134] In countries entangled in the complicated and multifaceted web of industrial development, a variety of factors can potentially heighten existing economic inequalities and create new ones. Unequal access to economically valuable goods due to social or political influence, especially those goods whose value rises along with the pace of industrialization, exacerbate differences in class standing, power, and prestige. The spread of commercialism across social and class lines polarizes competition over valued goods, especially those that are often in scarce supply, such as arable land and water. In instances where normative means of competition are lacking and there are permissive class structures and political circumstances, the potential for political violence is greatly magnified.

    Economic inequality can also arise from demographic growth, albeit indirectly, which similarly increases the scarcity of prized resources both in urban and in rural areas, particularly in the latter. Although the connection between the two developments is not universal, under certain circumstances population growth severely strains state capabilities and can bring it to the brink of collapse, as was the case immediately prior to the English revolution.[135] Reduction of state revenues and irregularities in finances, elite competition and turnover, and other negative ramifications that can arise out of population growth may in one way or another propel a weakened state stoward breakdown.[136] The connections among population growth, inequality, and revolutionary action is even more direct. "Given a finite set of resources, a bifurcation process takes place in which many persons have very little and a few persons have much. This process has been shown to occur in instances of mass revolution."[137] In fact, those revolutions that have involved the extensive mobilization of peasants have taken place in countries where there has been a scarcity of land and its concentration in strikingly few hands.[138]

The last category of economic grievances which can potentially lead to revolutionary mobilization stem from the predominance of particular class structures. These class-based mobilizational dynamics may or may not necessarily be exacerbated by the industrialization process. The prevalence of specific structures and patterns of intra- and interrelations within each class can significantly determine their potential for revolutionary mobilization. The middle and the lower classes, including the peasantry, are most directly amenable to grievances arising out of class structures and relations. As discussed earlier, the primary source of grievance among the middle classes is the frustration of their aspirations and feelings of relative deprivation.

Insofar as peasants and other rural inhabitants are concerned, their revolutionary mobilization is most feasible when the peasant community as a whole is strong and they enjoy some sort of economic and political autonomy, and when landlords or proxies of the establishment lack direct economic and political control at the local level.[139] Peasants with small holdings are normally conservative and quiescent, reluctant to risk losing their paltry goods and heavily dependent on rich peasants and landed upper classes.[140] Sharecroppers and propertyless laborers, who have little to loose and much to gain by risking the adversities of violent action, along with middle-income peasants frustrated by their inability to break into the ranks of large estate proprietors, are most apt to partake in revolutionary action. An equally inert conservatism similarly pervades over the upper echelons of the industrial working class, especially among highly skilled technical workers who form part of a "labor aristocracy."[141] Having finally secured stable and relatively comfortable positions, skilled industrial labourers are less willing to engage in the risky and often violent political activities in which the proletariat readily participate.

Despite their extremely important role, economic grievances are not the only category of dynamics that are conducive to mass mobilization. Society-wide grievances with deep roots among the population can arise out of the appearance of certain social and cultural factors as well. The many and varied ramifications of social change are examples of the developments that can propel an otherwise quiescent group of people into revolutionary mobilization. Socially-aroused political opposition is often attributed to an absence of "harmony" between a "society's values and the realities with which it must deal."[142] Disparities between the way people feel and behave and their surrounding environment may indeed lead to their disillusionment and the subsequent focusing of their anger on political targets. But, at least insofar as Third World countries are concerned, social antagonisms are more likely to arise out of an incoherence of the very values that people hold and cherish. Specifically, deeply-felt feelings of trauma and anguish are likely to occur when the prevailing values of society themselves are sharply divided, incoherent, and at times outright contradictory. Social and cultural homogeneity is hardly evident in any contemporary modern society. In some societies, however, especially those undergoing rapid modernization and development, values are so disjointed and contradictory that valuative heterogeneity turns into what are almost completely separate and unrelated clusters of different cultures. When sufficient numbers of people ascribe to these differing value systems, and they all demand equal shares of the available cultural and political resources, then there is potential for violent action, especially if normative means of political competition are nonexistent.

Yet the mutual incompatibility of desired and cherished values may not even transcend across social and class lines. People, especially citizens of Third World countries, who are constantly bombarded with ever-changing norms and values, can become disillusioned within themselves and in turn vent their anger on political objects. They become torn between the values that they have traditionally come to adopt and cherish and those contradictory ones which they either feel compelled to adopt or willingly desire.[143] The greater the intensity of the conflict among prevailing social values, the greater is the extent of individual and collective disillusionment, and thus the higher the probability of politically threatening behavior. Similarly, the more acutely aware of the conflict between the values to be adopted, the more disillusioned the average citizen feels and thus the greater likelihood of his or her political activism. That is primarily why in countries undergoing change and growth, students and intellectuals, whose job it is to examine prevailing social values, are more prone to political opposition than are other groups.[144]

Political Causes of Mass Mobilization

Lastly, a series of developments can give rise to politically-originated grievances. Because those grievances that are derived from social and economic developments are expressed in political terms, it is frequently difficult to distinguish between singularly political dynamics which prompt mass protests as opposed to those with social or economic roots. Nevertheless, there are a number of explicitly political developments which are by themselves sufficient causes for widespread political mobiliation. In fact, they are for the most part the same set of dynamics which bring about crises of legitimacy for incumbent elites and nullify their justifications for a continued hold on power. The same factors that lead to a regime's growing political weakness have the potential of bringing about mass mobilization. They include, among others, growing demands for greater political participation, increasing awareness of nationalist sentiments, and the widespread acceptance of ideologies other than that of the regime. There is, none the less, a fine and subtle difference between legitimacy crisis as such and politically-induced mass mobilization. Legitimacy crisis is one of the conditions through which states are weakened and are pushed to the verge of collapse. It is only then, well after a permissive political environment has appeared, that the same set of factors that had led to legitimacy crisis result in mass-based revolutionary mobilization.

A full examination of the grievances that provide the main impetus for mass mobilization is important not only in acquiring a more accurate picture of the causes of revolution but also in understanding the dynamics which result in the emergence of specific revolutionary leaders and their particular followers. The depth and preponderance of one particular form of grievance throughout society can by itself determine the composition of the revolution's leaders and their followers. More than anything else, the leaders and followers of a revolutionary movement are determined by the virtue of their relationship to the various sources of grievance that exist throughout society. Those who can most aptly discern the sources that aggrieve people, are ideologically and organizationally capable of exploiting this aggrievement, and offer either precise remedies or vague promises for their alleviation, rapidly ascend to leadership. At the same time, those masses who are most acutely afflicted with a certain form of actual or perceived misfortune, are organizationally and situationally most accessible to groups promising to alleviate those very misfortunes, and are emotionally and valuatively receptive to the appeals and cries of revolutionary leaders form the bulk of mobilized protestors. In short, the very dynamics which set revolution into motion to a great extent determine the character and nature of their leaders and followers.

It is precisely for this reason that the overwhelming participants of revolutions are made up of displaced and dispossessed peasants, disillusioned and unassimilated rural migrants, and the aspiring but frustrated segments of the middle classes. Given the right political circumstances, increased inequality and bifurcation due to growing scarcity or skewed commercialization can promote an appropriate environment within which peasants become politically active and mobilized. The discovery by self-proclaimed revolutionaries of the merits of peasant-based revolutions, derived either from practical realism or from doctrinal idealism, provides a nexus between the two groups that has been a recurrent feature of many contemporary Third World revolutions. The less-than-successful peasant-based revolutionary movements that flourish throughout Latin America at frequent pace attest to the centrality of the peasants-revolutionaries bond in causing considerable political havoc, if not necessarily outright revolution. The successful revolutions which occurred in China, Cuba, Vietnam, and to some extent in Nicaragua all did, none the less, entail considerable peasant participation.[145] At the same time, the cultural disillusionment, economic frustration, and political alienation of ever-growing proletariats turn them into readily-mobilizable foot-soldiers for various revolutionary causes, the full meanings of which they may not necessarily grasp or even endorse. Their participation in revolutionary movements is not so much a result of deep understanding of and adherence to specific revolutionary ideals but more a result of their readiness and availability, both emotionally and organizationally, to partake in politically oppositional activities. Those who do hold revolutionary hopes and aspirations and who do not hesitate to voice them are mostly drawn from among the ranks of the middle classes. By virtue of their social and economic positions, their education and background, and their political aspirations, the middle classes are much better positioned to assume the leadership mantle of a revolutionary movement, and when revolutions do occur, it is indeed the middle classes who are frequently in the forefront and are their most vociferous leaders. The politics of exactly what groups become mobilized and by whom are in turn determined by the prevailing social and cultural dynamics that bond the various social strata together.

CONCLUSION

Revolutions are clearly multifaceted phenomenon arising out of the interplay of an array of diverse political, economic, and social developments. They are, in the first place, products of skewed political development, of inherently unstable processes in which the body politic passes through, voluntarily or involuntarily, on its way toward becoming a modern polity. Revolutions are, in essence, violent struggles aimed at achieving a fuller and more developed political establishment that is supposedly more capable of delivering popularly desired goods and services than those which the present regime can offer. This struggle is in fact an eminently political one, with its genesis, direction, and scope and magnitude all dependent on the specific political configurations that happen to prevail at the time. However, the contextual environment within which the willful leaders and the receptive audience of this struggle emerge is heavily influenced by dynamics which may be fundamentally apolitical, particularly those that are social and cultural or economic in nature. The polarizing affects of this contextual environment are all the more accented in praetorian and contemporary Third World societies, where industrial development, rapid urbanization, and intense social change simultaneously take place at dizzying pace and breed an atmosphere that is highly conducive to the eruption of full-blown revolutions, or at least to the appearance of revolutionary movements.

The next chapter examines in detail the characteristic of post-revolutionary systems. Suffice it to say here that where revolutions lead is a question largely dependent on whether they are more planned in genesis and execution or involve greater spontaneity. Planned and spontaneous revolutions result in vastly different types of post-revolutionary systems, the latter based on previously formulated programs but the former being formed as the movement progresses. Each type of regime--more specifically, its emergent leaders and its institutions--evolves out of different sets of dynamics. Yet despite such dramatic differences in the *manner* of evolution and pattern of institutionalization, all post-revolutionary regimes have one common fundamental quality: all rely on and indeed thrive through the inclusion of the masses into the body politic.[146]

As mass-based movements from within society aimed at capturing political power, revolutions cannot evolve and succeed in inclusionary, populist regimes. As the next chapter demonstrates, opposition to post-revolutionary regimes can prove to be potentially far more costly, in human life if in nothing else, than that against regimes which are themselves product of a revolutionary experience. Nevertheless, political success in a revolution does not necessarily entail political stability. So long as normative means of political competition are absent, the tendency toward violence and revolution remain an endemic probability. Whether the new wave of emerging democracies in the Third World prove capable of stemming the tide of engendered instability remains to be seen. What is certain is the enduring likelihood of further revolutionary eruptions in narrowly-based, delegitimized regimes promoting rapid social change and industrial development in the face of non-responsive and unchangeable political structures.

Notes

1. For an examination of the concept of revolution, see James Farr, "Historical Concepts in Political Science: The Case of 'Revolution,'" *American Journal of Political Science* vol. 26, no. 4 (November 1982), pp. 688-708, and John Dunn, "Revolution," in T. Ball, J. Farr, and R. Hanson, eds., *Political Innovation and Conceptual Change* (Cambridge: Cambridge University Press, 1988).

2. John Dunn, *Modern Revolutions: An Introduction to the Analysis of a Political Phenomenon*, 2nd ed (Cambridge: Cambridge University Press, 1989), p. xvi.

3. Ibid.

4. Peter Calvert, *Politics, Power, and Revolution: An Introduction to Comparative Politics* (London: Wheatsheaf, 1983), p. 163.

5. See, for example, Laszlo Bruszt, "1989: The Negotiated Revolution in Hungary," *Social Research* vol. 51, no. 2 (Summer 1990), pp. 365-87.

6. Ibid, p. 386.

7. Mehran Kamrava, "Causes and Leaders of Revolutions,"*Journal of Social, Political, and Economic Studies* vol. 15, no. 1 (Spring 1990), p. 84.

8. A few examples of works on revolutions include: Michael Freeman, "Review Article: Theories of Revolution," *British Journal of Political Science* vol. 2, pp. 339-59; Rod Aya, "Theories of Revolution: Contrasting Models of Collective Violence," *Theory and Society* vol. 8, no. 1 (July 1979), pp. 39-99; Perez Zagorin, "Theories of Revolution in Contemporary Historiography," *Political Science Quarterly* vol. LXXXVIII, no. 1 (March 1973), pp. 23-52; Theda Skocpol, *States and Social Revolutions* (Cambridge: Cambridge University Press, 1979), Chap. 1; Issac Kromnick, "Reflections on Revolution: Definition and Explanation in Recent Scholarship," *History and Theory* vol. XI, no. 1 (1972), pp. 22-63; J.M. Maravall, "Subjective Conditions and Revolutionary Conflicts: Some Remarks," *British Journal of Sociology* vol. 27, no. 1 (March 1976), pp. 21-34; L. Stone, "Theories of Revolution," *World Politics* vol 18 (1966), pp. 159-76. Timothy Wickham-Crowley, "A Quantitative Comparative Approach to Latin American Revolutions," *International Journal of Comparative Sociology* vol. 32, nos. 1-2 (1991), pp. 82-109; and Wilber Chafee, "The Political Economy of Revolution and Democracy: Toward a

Theory of Latin American Politics," *The American Journal of Economics and Sociology* vol. 43, no. 4 (October 1984), pp. 385-99. For works in the "dependency" school of thought, see David Kowalewski, "Periphery Revolutions in World-System Perspective, 1821-1985," *Comparative Political Studies* vol. 24, no 1 (April 1991), pp. 76-99, and Terry Bosell and William Dixon, "Dependency and Rebellion: A Cross National Analysis," *American Sociological Review* vol 55 (August 1990), pp. 540-59.

9. See, especially, Barbara Salert, *Revolutions and Revolutionaries.* (New York: Elsevier, 1976), and Aya, "Theories of Revolution: Contrasting Models of Collective Violence".

10. Farr, "Historical Concepts in Political Science," p. 706.

11. Ibid.

12. John Dunn, *Rethinking Modern Political Theory* (Cambridge: Cambridge University Press, 1985), p. 77.

13. Kamrava, "Causes and Leaders of Revolutions," p. 84.

14. The Third World is inundated with examples of movements which embrace foreign ideologies and import them with little alteration to fit local conditions. "Maoist" groups across the Middle East and Latin America, especially the Shining Path in Peru, are prime examples.

15. Chalmers Johnson, *Revolutionary Change* (London: Longman, 1983).

16. James Davies, "Toward a Theory of Revolution," *American Sociological Review* vol. 27, no. 1 (February 1962), pp. 7-19. For a more updated elaboration of the same theme, though with greater emphasis on psychological factors, see James Davies, "Maslow and Theory of Political Development: Getting to Fundamentals," *Political Psychology* vol. 12, no. 3 (1991), pp. 389-420. See also, Ted Gurr, *Why Men Rebel?* (Princeton: Princeton University Press, 1970).

17. Samuel Huntington, *Political Order in Changing Societies* (New Haven, CT: Yale University Press, 1968).

18. Jerrold Green, "Counter Mobilization as a Revolutionary Form," *Comparative Politics* vol. 16, no. 2 (January 1984), pp. 153-69.

19. Skocpol, *States and Social Revolutions.*

20. Kamrava "Causes and Leaders of Revolutions," pp. 80-1.

21. See, for example, Theda Skocpol, "Rentier State and Shi'a Islam in the Iranian Revolution," *Theory and Society* vol. 11, no. 3 (May 1982), pp. 265-83.

22. Diplomatic pressures and conditional relations with the United States were highly instrumental in the direction and success of revolutions in Iran and the Philippines, as were relations between the Soviet Union and those governments which fell to revolutions in eastern Europe in the late 1980s.

23. Huntington, *Political Order in Changing Societies*, pp. 4-5.

24. Ibid, p. 168; for more on praetorian systems.

25. See Mehran Kamrava, *Politics and Society in the Third World* (London: Routledge, 1993), Chap. 4.

26. Edmond Keller, "Revolution and the Collapse of Traditional Monarchies: Ethiopia," Barry Schutz and Robert Slater, eds., *Revolution and Political Change in the Third World* (Boulder, CO: Lynne Rienner, 1990), p. 87.

27. Lucian Pye, "Legitimacy Crisis," Lucian Pye, et al., *Crises and Sequences in Political Development* (Princeton, NJ: Princeton University Press, 1971), p. 153.

28. Johnson, *Revolutionary Change*, p. 65.

29. Pye, "Legitimacy Crisis," Pye, et al., *Crises and Sequences*, p. 138.

30. Huntington, *Political Order in Changing Societies*, p. 31.

31. Pye, "Legitimacy Crisis," Pye et al., *Crises and Sequences*, p. 141.

32. Barry Schultz and Robert Slater, "A Framework for Analysis," Schultz and Slater, eds., *Revolution and Political Change in the Third World*, p. 5.

33. Pye, "Legitimacy Crisis," Pye et al., *Crises and Sequences*, p. 150.

34. Huntington, *Political Order in Changing Societies*, p. 275.

35. Jeff Goodwin and Theda Skocpol, "Explaining Revolutions in the Contemporary Third World," *Politics and Society* vol. 17, no. 4 (December 1989), p. 498.

36. See Kamrava, *State and Society in the Third World*, Chap. 1.

37. Goodwin and Skocpol, "Explaining Revolutions in the Contemporary Third World," pp. 498-9.

38. Ibid, p. 500.

39. See Kamrava. *State and Society in the Third World*, Chap. 1.

40. Barry Schultz and Robert Slater, "A Framework for Analysis," Schultz and Slater, eds., *Revolution and Political Change*, p. 7.

41. Barry Schultz and Robert Slater, "Patterns of Legitimacy and Future Revolutions in the Third World," Schultz and Slater, eds. *Revolution and Political Change*, p. 248.

42. See Kamrava. *Politics and Society in the Third World* Chap. 2.

43. Skocpol, *States and Social Revolutions*, p. 286.

44. Schultz and Slater, "A Framework for Analysis," p. 5.

45. Davies, "Toward a Theory of Revolution," p. 17.

46. Ted Gurr, *Why Men Rebel?* pp. 121-2.

47. R. Ben Jones, *The French Revolution* (London: Hodder & Stoughton, 1967), p. 16.

48. Richard Charques, *The Twilight of the Russian Empire* (Oxford:

Oxford University Press, 1965), p. 204.

49. Pedro Perez Sarduy, "Culture and the Cuban Revolution," *The Black Scholar* vol. 20, nos. 5-6 (Winter 1989), p. 18.

50. Mehran Kamrava, *Revolution in Iran: Roots of Turmoil* (London: Routledge, 1990), p. 68.

51. Bruszt, "1989: The Negotiated Revolution in Hungary," p. 386.

52. Jones, *The French Revolution*, p. 15.

53. Sarduy, "Culture and the Cuban Revolution," p. 19.

54. Kamrava, *Revolution in Iran*, p. 66.

55. Skocpol, *States and Social Revolutions*, p. 17.

56. Dunn, *Modern Revolutions*, p. xxi.

57. Skocpol, *States and Social Revolutions*, p. 31.

58. Ibid, p. 47.

59. See, especially, Huntington, *Political Order in Changing Societies*, Chap. 4, and Goodwin and Skocpol, "Explaining Revolutions in the Contemporary Third World," pp. 498-9.

60. Goodwin and Skocpol, "Explaining Revolutions in the Contemporary Third World," p. 504.

61. Ibid, p. 496.

62. David Mason, "Indigenous Factors," Schultz and Slater, eds. *Revolution and Political Change*, p. 40.

63. Goodwin and Skocpol. "Explaining Revolutions in the Contemporary Third World," p. 500.

64. Mason, "Indigenous Factors," Schultz and Slater eds., *Revolution and Political Change*, p. 33.

65. Kamrava, "Causes and Leaders of Revolutions," pp. 83-4.

66. See Kamrava, *Revolution in Iran*, pp. 30-2 and 40-5; and Bruszt, "1989: The Negotiated Revolution In Hungary," pp. 381-2.

67. Goodwin and Skocpol, "Explaining Revolutions in the Contemporary Third World," p. 501.

68. Schultz and Slater, "Patterns of Legitimacy and Future Revolutions in the Third World," Schultz and Slater, eds., *Revolution and Political Change*, p. 248.

69. Goodwin and Skocpol, "Explaining Revolutions in the Contemporary Third World," p. 502.

70. Foltz, "External Causes," Schultz and Slater, eds., *Revolution and Political Change*, pp. 54-9.

71. Gerard Chaliand, *Revolution in the Third World: Myths and Prospects* (New York: Viking Press, 1977), p. 40.

72. Foltz, "External Causes," Schults and Slater, eds., *Revolution and Political Change*, p. 63.

73. See Bruce Miroff, *Pragmatic Illusions: The Presidential Politics of John F. Kennedy* (New York: David McKay, 1976), especially pp. 110-

66. A more up-to-date discussion of U.S. foreign policy toward Latin America can be found in Thomas Paterson, J.G. Clifford, and Kenneth Hagan. *American Foreign Policy: A History* (Lexington, MA: D.C. Heath & Co., 1991), pp. 588-90 and 627-32.

74. Quoted in Clifford Krauss, "Revolution in Central America?" *Foreign Affairs* vol. 65, no. 3 (1987), p. 564.

75. Ibid, pp. 564-5.

76. Paterson, Clifford, and Hagan, *American Foreign Policy*, p. 588.

77. Huntington, *Political Order in Changing Societies*, p. 34.

78. See Kamrava, *State and Society in the Third World*, Chap. 1.

79. Huntington, *Political Order in Changing Societies*, p. 37.

80. Ibid, p. 56.

81. Ibid, p. 40.

82. Ibid, p. 21.

83. Irma Adelman and Jarius Hihn, "Crisis Politics in Developing Countries," *Economic Development and Cultural Change* vol. 33, no. 1 (October 1984), p. 20.

84. Elbaki Hermassi, *The Third World Reassessed* (Berkeley, CA: University of California Press, 1990), pp. 59-60.

85. Ibid, p. 44.

86. See Kamrava, *State and Society in the Third World*, Chap. 1.

87. For a discussion of "corporatism" see, Rod Hague and Martin Harrop, *Comparative Politics and Government: An Introduction* (Atlantic Highlands, NJ: Humanities Press, 1987), pp. 134-7. See also above, Chap. 1.

88. Goodwin and Skocpol, "Explaining Revolutions in the Contemporary Third World," p. 500.

89. Dunn, *Rethinking Modern Political Theory*, p. 77.

90. Dunn, *Modern Revolutions*, p. 236.

91. In *Political Order in Changing Societies*, Samuel Huntington classifies revolutions into "Eastern" and "Western" ones (p. 266).

92. Planned revolutions correspond closely to the variety Robert Dix calls "Latin American." Such revolutions occur, he writes, "in regimes that have been narrow, modernizing, military-based dictatorships rather than, say, weak monarchies. They have not simply collapsed, almost of their own weight, as in the Western style of revolution. Instead, they have had to be overthrown and their supporting armed forces defeated or demoralized in combat with those bent on revolution." Robert Dix, "Varieties of Revolution," *Comparative Politics* vol. 15, no. 3 (April 1983), p. 283.

93. Goodwin and Skocpol, "Explaining Revolutions in the Contemporary Third World," p. 492.

94. Carlos Vilas, "Popular Insurgency and Social Revolution in

Central America," *Latin American Perspectives* vol. 15, no. 1 (Winter 1988), p. 69.

95. Ibid, p. 70.

96. James Scott, "Hegemony and the Peasantry," *Politics and Society* vol. 7, no. 3 (1977), p. 294.

97. Theda Skocpol, "What Makes Peasants Revolutionary?" *Comparative Politics* vol. 14, no. 3 (April 1982), p. 364.

98. Scott, "Hegemony and the Peasantry," p. 295.

99. Chaliand, *Revolution in the Third World*, p. 48.

100. Ibid, pp. 42-3.

101. Huntington, *Political Order in Changing Societies*, p. 290.

102. Goodwin and Skocpol, "Explaining Revolutions in the Contemporary Third World," p. 496.

103. Chaliand, *Revolution in the Third World*, p. 35.

104. Stuart Schram, *The Political Thought of Mao Tse Tung* (New York: Praeger, 1972), p. 253. See also, ibid, pp. 236-64.

105. Scott, "Hegemony and the Peasantry," p. 289.

106. Eric Wolf, *Peasant Wars of the Twentieth Century* (New York: Harper & Row, 1969), p. 276.

107. Ibid, p. 279. Also see Skocpol, "What Makes Peasants Revolutionary?".

108. Goodwin and Skocpol, "Explaining Revolutions in the Contemporary Third World," p. 497.

109. Mason, "Indigenous Factors," p. 42.

110. Goodwin and Skocpol, "Explaining Revolutions in the Contemporary Third World," p. 493.

111. Ibid.

112. Jerrold Green, "Countermobilization as a Revolutionary Form," p. 147.

113. Ibid, pp. 160-1.

114. Johnson, *Revolutionary Change*, p. 101.

115. This was precisely the case in the revolutions that occurred in France, Iran, and in Eastern Europe in the end of the 1980s. In the Russian revolution, however, the soviets played an important organizational role.

116. Chaliand, *Revolution in the Third World*, p. 40.

117. See Kamrava, *Revolution in Iran*, Chap. 5, esp. pp. 128-30; for Eastern Europe, see the special edition on Eastern European revolutions in *Social Research* vol. 57, no. 2 (Summer 1990).

118. Thomas Greene, *Contemporary Revolutionary Movements*. (Englewood Cliffs, NJ: Prentice-Hall, 1974), p. 57.

119. This was particularly the case in the Cuban and the Ethiopian revolutions, where the ideological orientations of post-revolutionary

political leaders did not fully become apparent until some time after their success.

120. Goodwin and Skocpol, "Explaining Revolutions in the Contemporary Third World," p. 494.

121. Huntington, *Political Order in Changing Societies*, pp. 300-1.

122. Greene, *Contemporary Revolutionary Movements*, p. 63.

123. Mason, "Indigenous Factors," p. 48.

124. Ibid, p. 44.

125. Barrington Moore, *Injustice: The Social Base of Obedience and Revolt* (London: Macmillan, 1978), p. 459.

126. Calvert, *Politics, Power, and Revolution*, p. 168.

127. See Kamrava, *State and Society in the Third World*, Chap. 2.

128. Gurr, *Why Men Rebel?*, pp. 121-2.

129. Davies, "Toward a Theory of Revolution," p. 8.

130. Gurr, *Why Men Rebel?*, p. 46. For a full analysis of relative deprivation see ibid, pp. 46-56.

131. Ibid, p. 37.

132. Ibid, p. 205.

133. Manus Midlarsky, "Rulers and the Ruled: Patterned Inequality and the Onset of Mass Political Violence," *American Political Science Review* vol. 82, no. 2 (July 1988), p. 492.

134. Ibid, p. 493.

135. See Jack Goldstone, "State Breakdown in the English Revolution: A New Synthesis," *American Journal of Sociology* vol. 92, no. 2 (September 1986), pp. 257-322.

136. Ibid, pp. 310-11.

137. Manus Midlarsky, "Scarcity and Inequality: Prologue to the Onset of Mass Revolution," *Journal of Conflict Resolution* vol. 26, no. 1 (March 1982), p. 34.

138. Midlarsky, "Rulers and the Rule," pp. 493-4.

139. Jerome Himmelstein and Michael Kimmel, "Review Essay: States and Revolutions: The Implications and Limits of Skocpol's Structural Model," *American Journal of Sociology* vol. 86, no. 5 (March 1981), p. 1147. Also see Theda Skocpol. "What Makes Peasants Revolutionary?".

140. Jeffrey Paige, *Agrarian Revolution: Social Movements and Export Agriculture in the Underdeveloped World*, (New York: Free Press, 1975), p. 41.

141. Val Moghadam, "Industrial Development, Culture, and Working-Class Politics: A Case Study of Tabriz Industrial Workers in the Iranian Revolution," *International Sociology* vol. 2, no. 2 (June 1987), pp. 164-5.

142. Johnson, *Revolutionary Change*, p. 62.

143. See Kamrava, *State and Society in the Third World*, Chap. 2.
144. Huntington, *Political Order in Changing Societies*, p. 290.
145. See Dunn, *Modern Revolutions*.
146. See below, pp. 73-4.

3

Post-Revolutionary States

A discussion of post-revolutionary states must necessarily entail an examination of the point at which revolutions are thought to have succeeded. This is a risky venture for the success of revolutions is, by their very nature, elusive and almost impossible to pinpoint. The question of exactly when revolutions succeed has historically depended more on the proclamations of new political governors and actors, claiming to have achieved at least the most pivotal goal of the revolution--the attainment of power--rather than intricate academic theorizing in search of a specific event or development *within* the post-revolutionary regime which would signify the revolution's ultimate success or failure. Did the French, Russian, Chinese, Cuban, and the Iranian revolutions, to name just a few, succeed when previously revolutionary groups assumed power and became the state themselves, or when these new leaders achieved some avowedly revolutionary goal, such as a classless or an Islamic society, *after* gaining control over the reins of power? Did the Russian revolution succeed in October 1917 or, as indeed a credible argument can be made, is it still continuing?[1] Similarly, differing dates and points of success can be forwarded for almost all other historic revolutions.[2]

The question becomes even more puzzling when revolutionary leaders are taken at their word, for they often see their revolution as an on-going, continuous process whose success depends on the workings of as-yet subdued dynamics. For the vast majority of leaders of post-revolutionary states, particularly those who took active part in the revolutionary struggle, the revolution never ends. Whether due to political prudence or a matter of genuine commitment, for the likes of Lenin, Mao, and Khomeini the end of the revolution never came, the fruition of their ultimate dreams and ideals having been superseded by their own deaths.[3] Fidel Castro's fiery speeches and his unendingly passionate stewardship of Cuba epitomize more than just bombastic rhetoric. They give insight into his conviction that the Cuban revolution is still continuing. Historians may chose different dates to denote the end of one era and the start of another. But at least as far as revolutionary leaders are concerned, revolutions never end. It is often only with the coming to fore of second- and third-generation revolutionary leaders, the children and disciples of the original victors of power, that the fervor of revolutionary continuity eventually simmers down and gives way to a routine pattern of political conduct.

Yet even before the ascension of new generations of leaders, revolutions are seen to have fully succeeded when the political sentiments to which they have given rise are translated into actual political arrangements, successfully superimposed on existing ones. In her analysis of the French, Russian, and Chinese revolutions, Theda Skocpol found that they "were fully consummated only once new state organizations--administrations and armies, coordinated by executives who governed in the name of revolutionary symbols--were built up amidst the conflicts of revolutionary situations."[4] "In all three revolutionary situations," she argues,

> political leaderships and regimes--the Jacobins and then the Napoleonic in France, the Bolshevik in Russia, and the Communist in China--emerged to reestablish national order, to consolidate the socioeconomic transformation wrought by the class upheavals from below, and to enhance each country's power and autonomy over and against international competitors.[5]

It is with such post-revolutionary regimes--those embedded in new symbols and entrusted with new tasks, products of movements from within society to capture state and to thereby alter its conduct and nature--that the present chapter is concerned. It is concerned with the establishment and conduct of new institutional arrangements, and the nature and initiatives of emergent political leaders following the collapse of the Old Order. The success of revolutionary movements in capturing political power, whether they are planned or spontaneous, turns the world of politics around. The mandate of government changes, leaders having promised a universe of new realities and followers having risked their lives for those promises. Upon seizure of power, the revolutionary project is itself at once revolutionized: no longer is the task one of achieving state paralysis but rather one of consolidation. Political power, once the focus of anger and anti-government sentiments, is now the embodiment of the ideals for which the masses rose. It is now entrusted with establishing its promised world. Its leaders and their agendas, its institutions and their organs, its ideals and their audience, and the manner and the means with which it conducts itself are all products of a revolutionary struggle, one in which the world of politics was turned upside down. The day now belongs to a new cadre of leaders. Their concern is not only to carve out a new national identity, to create the ideal society in which they invested the hopes of the masses, but at the same time to popularly legitimize their rule and live up to their revolutionary rhetoric. Their efforts are thus directed at augmenting the various linkages and nexes between the state and society, incorporating the popular strata into the process of government, and concurrently solidifying their own hold on power through institutional consolidation and political centralism.

Ironically, in their attempt to forge a new society and make good on their revolutionary promises, post-revolutionary states often inadvertently accentuate economic hardships. The economically redistributive character of most revolutionary states, despite the loudly-proclaimed goals of the actors involved, do not always enhance the economic lot of their target audience. Indeed, as will be shown, the results are often the opposite. It is with these characteristics of post-revolutionary states--their leaders and their sources of legitimacy, popular political participation and institutional centralism, and the economic dynamics involved--which the present chapter is concerned.

LEADERSHIP

The success of the revolutionary struggle brings to the fore a new cadre of leaders, men (and, in a few instances, women) for whom the revolutionary project now becomes one of governing rather than capturing and destroying. Who are these men and why do they emerge as the revolution's eventual or temporary victors? And, why, as is often the case, do some leaders of post-revolutionary states show greater resilience in political stewardship than others? The question of who assumes the leadership of the post-revolutionary state greatly depends on the nature of the revolutionary movement and the manner in which the revolutionary drama succeeded in overturning the established order.

Planned Versus Spontaneous Revolutions and Post-Revolutionary Leadership

Specifically, insofar as the leadership composition of post-revolutionary states are concerned, the rise of specific actors to leadership positions depends on whether a revolution was planned or spontaneous.[6] In planned revolutions, the leadership of the post-revolutionary state is assumed by leaders of the guerrilla organization which spearheaded the struggle against the old order. Without exception, in successful, guerrilla-fought (and thus planned) revolutions, yesterday's rebels become today's leaders. History provides numerous examples of successful guerrilla revolutions in which post-revolutionary leaders were drawn from the ranks of the guerrilla organization. Mao and other leaders of the Chinese Communist party subsequently assumed leadership of China's post-revolutionary, communist state. Similarly, leaders of those states which emerged from the Algerian, Cuban, and Vietnamese revolutions were those who had been directly involved in leading the revolutionary fight.[7] Unlike leaders of spontaneous revolutions, these former guerrillas have for the most part shown remarkable resilience in holding on to power in post-revolutionary states.

The emergence of post-revolutionary leaders in spontaneous revolutions takes a slightly different course, although the underlying dynamics which lead to their accession are not fundamentally different from those at work in planned revolutions. Those who rise to leadership positions after the success of spontaneous revolutions are also figures once prominent in the revolutionary movement. Their ultimate success and survivability in the post-revolutionary era is, however, less predictable and depends on evolving and changeable circumstances and dynamics. Consequently, leaders who eventually come to claim the leadership mantle of states that have emerged from spontaneous revolutions are often not the same as those who gave direction and provided leadership for the amorphous revolutionary movement. In these instances, the assumption of post-revolutionary leadership depends on the characteristics, qualifications, and situational opportunities of the individual personalities themselves, as well as on prevailing social and political dynamics. Before examining in detail the forces instrumental in the shaping of post-revolutionary states in both spontaneous and planned revolutions, an analysis of alternative explanations of revolutionary outcomes is in order.

Brinton: The Rise of the Extremists

"The revolution, like Saturn, devours its children."[8] So is the dominant theme of Crane Brinton's pioneering work on revolutionary outcomes, arguing that the initial victory of revolutionary leaders is but a brief "honeymoon" by relative moderates before themselves being overthrown by the "illegal government" of extremists. Revolutions follow an almost unilinear path, starting with the honeymoon of the moderates, moving on to a Reign of Terror, eventually settling down during a "Thermodorian" reaction, "a period of convalescence from the fever of revolution."[9] "There is a tendency," Brinton argues,

> for power to go from Right to Center to Left, from the conservatives of the old regime to the moderates to the radicals or extremists. As power moves along this line, it gets more and more concentrated, more and more narrow, its base in the country and among the people, since at each important crisis the defeated group has to drop out of politics.[10]

The consolidation of power by extremists is brought on by their superior organizational skills and their greater ability to fight foreign and domestic wars, which, Brinton claims, are natural derivatives of revolutionary movements.[11] In an environment polarized by "heated debates, attempted repression, (and) a steady stream of violent propaganda," the extremists find the political arena particularly hospitable to their own ends.[12] These are "heaven-storming idealists, scornful of compromise," disciplined ideologues particularly adept in dealing with crises.[13] They have all the means and the determination which their moderate counterparts lack. Their ultimate victory, however, often comes in the form of a *coup d'etat*, a final *putsch* through which the "illegal government" capitalizes on the incapacitation of the moderates and establishes itself as the sole, legitimate heir of the revolution.[14] Yet their reign is impermanent, for "most men cannot long stand the strains of prolonged effort to live in accordance with high ideals."[15] Eventually, "after a revolution has undergone a crisis and the accompanying centralization of power, some strong leader must handle the centralized power when that mad religious energy of the crisis has burned itself out."[16] Oliver Cromwell, Napoleon Bonaparte, and Josef Stalin were more than mere men of ambition. They fit into a specific pattern in post-revolutionary states, epitomizing centralized power and a semblance of return to social and political normalcy.[17]

Skocpol: Class and Structure

More recent studies of revolutionary outcomes have been less deterministic. By far the most thorough attempt at constructing an analytical framework for the study of revolutions and their outcomes is that of Theda Skocpol, who originally concentrated on class and structural dynamics as pivotal forces in determining the character of post-revolutionary states. While recognizing the importance of revolutionary ideologies and popular commitment to them as one of the "necessary ingredients" of major, historical revolutions, Skocpol argued that the "cognitive content of the ideologies in (no) sense proved a predictive key to either the outcomes of the Revolutions or the activities of the revolutionaries who built the state organizations that consolidated the Revolutions."[18] Instead, "ideologically oriented leaderships in revolutionary crises have been greatly limited by existing structural conditions and severely buffeted by the rapidly changing currents of revolutions."[19] Two specific sets of factors, the structural circumstances within which revolutionary struggles are waged and the features and relations of the various classes, determine the ultimate outcome of revolutionary episodes.

> Revolutionary struggles have emerged from crises of state and class domination, and social-revolutionary outcomes have been powerfully shaped by the obstacles and opportunities offered by those crises. Likewise, social-revolutionary outcomes have been shaped and limited by the existing socioeconomic structures and international circumstances within which revolutionary leaderships have struggled to rebuild, consolidate, and use state power. . . . Variations in revolutionary conflict and outcome (can be) explained partly in terms of the specific features of each revolutionary crisis: exactly how each old-regime state broke apart; exactly what kinds of peasant revolts were facilitated by existing agrarian structures. And variations (can be) also . . . explained partly by reference to the specific socioeconomic structures and international situations carried over, more or less from each old to new regime. . . . [E]xplanations of the conflicts and outcomes of socialrevolutions best flow . . . of the prior understanding of the structuresand situations of old regimes and from a prior analysis of the causes of social-revolutionary crises. Revolutionary changes are accomplished upon such foundations and within such circumstances.[20]

Skocpol continues to assert that

> both the occurrence of the revolutionary situations in the first place and the nature of the New Regimes that emerged from the revolutionary conflicts depended fundamentally upon the structures of state organizations and their partially autonomous and dynamic relationships to domestic class and political forces, as well as their positions to other states abroad. [21]

While Skocpol's analysis significantly enhanced the understanding of revolutionary eruptions and outcomes, her strict emphasis on pre-revolutionary, structural arrangements as determinants of outcomes of revolutions was soon challenged by others and revised by herself. Structural and class dynamics may indeed be of paramount importance in certain revolutions. However, as the Iranian revolution so starkly demonstrated, forces other than the structural and class arrangements of pre-revolutionary states, such as culture and newly-emerging organizational capabilities, may prove to be just as equally important in determining the leaders of post-revolutionary states.

Skocpol Amended: Process and Culture

As a result, an analytical framework somewhat different from Skocpol's was forwarded. S.N. Eisenstadt, whose discussions in this vein are among the most elaborate, argues that revolutionary outcomes are

> not necessarily given in the pre-revolutionary structure of society but . . . the product of interaction among pre-revolutionary characteristics, the forces of change--most notably, international forces--and the revolutionary process itself. Only through such interaction do coalitions of broad classes and coalitions between them and their major types of institutional entrepreneurs arise and change.[22]

In a later article, Skocpol sharpened the focus of her original analysis of revolutionary outcomes. She argued that

> to understand which political leadership will win out in (at least the initial stages of) the consolidation of state power in a social- revolutionary situation, one must ask *not* which leaders are most "modern" by some Western or technical standard, but which possess, or can easily develop within given historical circumstances, the appropriate political resources.[23] (original emphasis)

At the same time, concurrent with her greater attention to the importance of access to specific political resources, Skocpol argued that there may well exist "moral symbols and forms of social communication" which *may* result in a culture conducive to challenges to authority. These cultural dynamics warrant greater attention in certain revolutions, such as the one in Iran, where the role and contribution of cultural forces to the revolution's overall character and ultimate outcome are irrefutable. [24]

The analytical approaches of all three authors discussed here find partial or complete applicability to the historic examples that they set out to examine. Brinton, a historian, carefully charts his discussion of the revolutionary moderates's "honeymoon," the emerging "crisis of extremists," and the subsequent "thermidorian reaction" by analyzing the English, American, French, and Russian revolutions.[25] Skocpol similarly examines the French, Russian, Chinese, and later the Iranian revolution with considerable skill and historical accuracy.[26] Eisenstadt's analysis involves less overt reliance on historical examples and is more thematic, his primary concern being the overall nature of post-revolutionary states rather than the particularities of their leaderships.[27] All approaches are credible scholarly explicandums for the study of outcomes of revolutions, at least in so far as the *political structures* of post-revolutionary states are concerned, and illuminate facets of analysis previously unexplored.

Nevertheless, in one way or another they mostly leave certain specific questions about the nature of post-revolutionary leadership unanswered. Specifically, the issue of exactly how the "moderates" (to use Brinton's term) or the initial victors of the revolutionary struggle assume power is at best treated with scant attention.[28] Only Skocpol mentions, in passing, that "during revolutionary interregnums, political leaderships rise and fall according to how successful they are in creating and using political arrangements within the crisis circumstances that they face." She continues:

> Struggles over the most fundamental issues of politics and state forms go on until relatively new state organizations have been consolidated; thereafter political struggles continue about how to use state power

in its broadly established forms.[29]

While these lines of analysis may not necessarily be inaccurate, they do not adequately deal with the questions of exactly how and why specific individuals ascend to leadership positions in post-revolutionary states while others do not. What is necessary is an analytical framework which discusses not only the overall characteristics of post-revolutionary states, as those discussed above do, but which also takes into account the nature and character of forces which lead to the emergence of particular leaders. It is here, in examining post-revolutionary leaderships as well as revolutionary causes and processes, that a distinction between planned and spontaneous revolutions further demonstrates its analytical utility. Leaders of successful planned revolutions almost invariably end up leading the states that emerge subsequent to their victory. This almost-assured ascendance arises from the fact that guerrilla-based revolutions are largely battles between competing organizations, struggles involving the organized forces of the government versus disciplined and armed guerrilla organizations. When the government's forces are defeated and its organizational apparatuses are captured, the only viable organisations through which political power could be exercised are at the disposal of the former guerrillas, who, by their very nature as members of a guerrilla organization, are adept at utilizing and manipulating organizational procedures, command structures, and policy-making mechanisms. It is important to remember that in pre-revolutionary societies, the establishment and activism of guerrilla organizations are intended to bring together otherwise disparate and uncoordinated political tendencies. The aim is to forge institutional venues for political expression and mobilization in settings where such institutions either do not exist altogether or if they do, they operate under tight government control. Thus during and immediately after the revolutionary struggle, guerrilla organizations are the only viable means through which popularly legitimized political power can be exercised. As a result, guerrilla leaders become heads of the newly-emerging political establishment. The consolidation and monopolization of power by all post-revolutionary states merely reinforces the political survival of former guerrillas as new political bosses.

The emergence of leaders following successful spontaneous revolutions, in which disciplined and organized political parties by and large do not play an overwhelming role, follows a path different from that in planned revolutions. Before revolutionary victory, leaders of spontaneous revolutions emerge relatively late in the movement, when the anti-regime struggle has already gotten underway, albeit in an uncoordinated and amorphous fashion. This ascendence, as discussed in the previous chapter, is facilitated by both the cultural communicability of the emerging leaders's ideology in relation to the larger society, in addition to the means of access they have, either in the form of formal organizations or by virtue of their social positions, through which they can communicate with large numbers of people in a relatively free manner. However, unless in the post-revolutionary era they give political substance and organizational solidity to their largely culturally-derived position, they will not be able to maintain themselves as leaders of the post-revolutionary state. Culturally compatible ideologies and access to means of mass mobilization are important in mustering support against a regime. These factors do not lose their importance in the post-revolutionary state, but for them to bear actual political fruit they now need to be transformed into institutional means of exercising state power, means which can help achieve explicitly political ends and objectives. What is important, in Skocpol's words, "is that which political leaderships in revolutionary crises are above all *doing*--claiming and struggling to maintain state power."[30] (original emphasis)

Consolidation by Organization

Here the role of political organisations and institutions established immediately prior to or right after revolutionary victory assume particular importance, especially if their establishment took place with an eye toward wresting political power from other, competing centers. The collapse of the *ancien régime* and the resulting release of revolutionary energies give rise to a multiplicity of groups and organizations seeking to reap maximum benefits from the emerging political vacuum. Not unlike pre-revolutionary times, when the mobilizational abilities of groups determined their leadership viability, the abilities of the different groups to mobilize the most numerous and dedicated of followers in the post-revolutionary environment is also instrumental in facilitating their ascension to leadership of the emerging regime. However, precisely because the organizational apparatuses of the former regime are no longer viable due to their defeat in the revolutionary struggle, especially the armed forces and the bureaucracy, the new political aspirants need to have at least comparable if not stronger organizations at their own disposal in order to establish effective, society-wide political control. It is access and control to these "appropriate political resources"[31] which ultimately determines the leaders of spontaneous revolutions.

The conflict between the Girondins and the Jacobins, both of whom claimed to be the rightful heirs of the French revolution, was eventually settled in favour of the latter only after they had placed themselves at the helm of the *sans-cullotes*.[32] The Jacobin's cultivation of ties with these revolutionary foot-soldiers was at times reluctant, the latter fearing the consequences of too close of an alliance with the former, who were at times too fanatical in their adherence to moral purity and revolutionary fervor.[33] Nevertheless, the *sans-cullotes* proved an invaluable weapon whose manipulation and leadership by the Jacobins greatly facilitated the establishment of the Committee of Public Safety and the era that has since come to be known as the Reign of Terror.[34] The Bolsheviks's leadership of Russia's revolutionary movement and of the emerging governing apparatus was largely the result of their extensive control of the soviets, thus giving them significant organizational leverage compared to other revolutionary competitors.[35] At the same time, their patronage of the peasantry, epitomized by Lenin's program of "Peace and Bread, Peace and Land," one based either on political opportunism or genuine concern, added to the Bolsheviks's supporters an increasingly important segment of Russia's revolutionized society.[36] In the Iranian revolution, the clerical establishment, one among the many groups that had in one way or another "led" the revolution, quickly used its wide popular support base to gain control of the many local revolutionary committees (the *komitehs*) and the irregular militia calling themselves revolutionary guards (*Pasdaran-e*

Enghelab) which had sprang up throughout the country soon after the collapse of the shah's regime.[37] Soon the Islamic Republic Party was established, giving organizational viability and cohesion to the clergy's populist ascent to power.[38] The outcome of the Nicaraguan revolution, which fell somewhere in between the planned and the spontaneous models, was largely the result of widespread and grass-roots support for the principal revolutionary party, the FSLN, and its affiliated organizations at the expense of potential rivals.[39]

In all these examples, the determining factors were both organizational and political: leaders became leaders because of access to organizations and institutions through which they could communicate with their respective revolutionary audiences. These very organizations soon became significant administrative arms of the states that were subsequently established, those at their helm or those who claimed to speak on their behalf becoming leaders of that state. For those who did not have access to equally strong organizations, or who saw no need for organizations of any sort at all, political leadership became less and less of a lasting reality, particularly as the revolutionary process continued to steam ahead.

It is here where Brinton's assertions of revolutions eating their own children and of the overthrow of moderates by the "illegal government" of extremists assumes greater clarity. Revolutions, at least in their immediate aftermath, result in an atmosphere of uncertainty and competition, in an uncapping of forces long suppressed and eager to make their political mark. At their height, when the regime is weakest and its opponents the loudest, revolutions have numerous self-proclaimed leaders, men (women have been historically absent from the scene) of different ideological persuasions, skills, and political purchase. It is those with the most viable, emerging institutions at their disposal, political, military, and otherwise--revolutionary committees and ad hoc organizations, self-appointed policemen and irregular militia--who are able to hegemonize the institutional mechanisms used for governing society and as a result usurp the revolution, justly or unjustly, in their own favor. These are pragmatist politicos, hardened by the realities of trying to govern a society made ungovernable by the tumults of revolution. They are men adept at praxis, aware of those intricate nuances of

daily life which assume such overwhelming significance in
extraordinary circumstances of the magnitude of revolutions.
They are, by nature, different from the well-meaning idealists
who were, along with others, vociferously heard from in the
earlier phases of the revolution. In comparison, the intellectuals,
"the moderates," as Brinton calls them,[40] are overly
philosophical in orientation and temperament, men more of
letters than the sword. Their concern is with generalities, the
overall quality of the new universe which the revolution has
brought about, not with the details of political organization.[41]
Their affinity with cold, pragmatic concerns often translates into
more than merely superior organizational abilities. It often
manifests itself in the form of a lack of compunction about the
violent use of terror in attaining short-term results. "The logic of
the situation," writes one observer,

> imposes a kind of ruthless eliminatory struggle on the
> participants. One can see this re-enactment in any
> society in which a revolution destroys the old
> recognized center of legitimacy and the old circle of
> mutually reinforcing convention: competing new self-
> proclaimed authorities emerge, none of which is yet
> hallowed by age. The one which can destroy or
> intimidate the other most effectively eventually
> concentrates power in its own hand.[42]

That this endemic eagerness to use violence later leads to an
unprecedented level of political centralization in post-
revolutionary states will be discussed later. But in so far as the
more idealistic, moderate elements are concerned, it is not
surprising that they find their political space increasingly
narrowed in the post-revolutionary government, eventually so
much so that they cease in any way to be a part of it. Brinton's
assertion of revolutions moving from the extreme right to center to
the extreme left[43] is less a historically natural pattern of
revolutions and more a product of the political and institutional
resources at the disposal of one of the revolution's initially many
victors. Nevertheless, as most revolutionary experiences have
demonstrated, there is a tendency in post-revolutionary
governments to use violence, often in generous portions, as a

necessary end to reach higher ideals. The first victims of such violence, sanctioned as it is by clusters of leaders within the evolving state, are those inside the establishment who begin to question the merits of these higher goals and agendas, revolutionaries who do not necessarily agree with the direction in which the revolution is going. They pose the most potent threat. Their stature and popularity has been enhanced by their participation in the revolutionary struggle, their ideologies and dogma having at least some support and appeal among those who poured into the streets. They are, indeed, the children of the revolution, placed in the unfortunate position of being unable to contain it to their own liking and thus falling to its wrath.

But just as the leadership of the post-revolutionary state becomes clearer, so is the New Society that it leads cleansed of non-conformist threats. After the state has filtered out its ideologically less-reliable elements, then the focus of political correctness shifts to society. The new regime seeks to subdue actual or perceived threats by clamping down on politically excluded groups, those with doctrinal tendencies different from the regime's increasingly all-encompassing world view. One after another, political parties are banned, free-thinking intellectuals harassed, and dissenters terrorized. All of these developments, from the relatively speedy emergence of consolidated groups within the broad coalition of revolutionary leaders to the brutal campaigns of social purification, are efforts which, purposefully or not, expedite the institutionalization of the new order. They point to the political coming of age of the revolutionary establishment, a process whereby the tenuous hold of new leaders becomes solidified, their supporting institutions are strengthened, and the impermanence of their revolution becomes permanent. It is to these developments which we next turn.

INSTITUTIONALIZATION

Clearly, one of the most pressing problems of post-revolutionary states is that of routinization, one of converting destructive collective revolutionary energies into politically constructive tasks. Having eliminated potential sources of competition, the new leaders of the emerging state now turn their attention to strengthening and augmenting the institutional mechanisms through which they rule. These new institutions, and the ground rules which govern their conduct and their relationship with the larger society, form the very basis of post-revolutionary states.[44] The primary task of the holders of power becomes one of consolidating and institutionalizing it.[45] This they achieve through accumulating as much power as possible, enhancing the centralized features of new state apparatuses, inculcating a new sense of legitimacy and shaping new perceptions of political and national identity, and incorporating the popular classes into the political process. Rhetoric, terror, and brutality do not necessarily subside but are complemented by various organizations designed to perpetuate the new order and to provide direction and substance to the wishes of the new elite.

Reinforcing the need for new organizations and other institutional means of support is the impermanent nature of charismatic authority, on which the legitimacy of most revolutionary states is at least initially based. Charisma is an inherently unstable form of authority, eventually giving way to routinized forms of political conduct.[46] At some point in the life of post-revolutionary states, the charismatic foundation on which the regime's legitimacy is based, one derived from the efforts of specific figures during the revolutionary struggle, will sooner or later wane due to natural deaths or political purges.[47] Even if the charismatic leader continues to remain at the helm of the post-revolutionary state, as is for example the case of Fidel Castro and the Cuban state, the need to complement charismatic appeal with actual political apparatuses soon becomes apparent. Thus even during the active leaderships of charismatic, revolutionary founding fathers in the Soviet Union, Cuba, and Iran, for example, political parties and affiliated organizations were created with the specific aim of institutionally enhancing the rule of the state.[48]

Moreover, the popular excitement generated as a result of the revolution is bound to subside at some point, even in instances when domestic revolutions spill over into international wars and result in a tremendous outpouring of nationalist sentiments. The new regime cannot count on an indefinite expression of enthusiasm by the popular classes as a viable source of sustenance. With extra-institutional sources of authority being by nature impermanent, specific organizations which will perpetuate the longevity of the new order assume particular importance. In fact, post-revolutionary elites often view their survival as dependent on their control not only of new organizations but of other, previously autonomous ones. Organizations involving the military, youth, culture, religion, education, and the economy are either all brought under the regime's direct influence, or, if previously non-existent, are established anew for that specific purpose.[49]

The overall nature of emerging post-revolutionary institutions, as well as the manner of their conduct, largely depend on whether the revolutions that bring them about are more planned in genesis and execution or involve greater spontaneity. Planned revolutions are based largely on premeditated programs devised by willful revolutionaries who know precisely what they want and have a clear idea of the ways and means to achieve their goals. Their efforts are undertaken with clear goals in mind and, if successful, there is thus often little disparity between their previously proclaimed goals--apart, of course, from their boisterous and at times manipulative and false promises--and newly-initiated policies. Spontaneous revolutions, on the other hand, are more often the outcome of developments that at first look hardly revolutionary. They involve neither formulated programs nor planned initiatives. Their leaders emerge relatively late, and the ultimate goals of those leaders are formed and pronounced even later. The revolution's goals and ideals are initially elusive at best, summed up in dogmatic slogans and vague promises. Each cadre of leaders promises such appealing alternatives as democracy and equality, principles that are left open to differing interpretations once it is time for their implementation. In these instances, the ideals and purposes of revolutions often appear vastly contradictory to their eventual outcomes, a contradiction which is more the result of the inherent looseness of the revolutionary process itself rather than the sinister manipulation of revolutionary turn-faces.

Nevertheless, with remarkable uniformity and regardless of whether spontaneous or planned, revolutions give rise to populist, inclusionary regimes.[50] By nature, revolutions involve the patronage of masses of people. The relationship between revolutionary leaders and followers is essentially one of patrons and clients, with the group most capable of catering to the needs and wishes of the widest spectrum of people emerging as their leader in opposing the establishment. Once the revolution has succeeded and formerly oppositional leaders become newly-seated elites, their reliance on the patronage of the masses does not wither and is in fact in most instances accentuated. Their mandate is no longer to oppose the regime but to make good on the numerous promises they gave before the revolution's success. The viability of the fledgling post-revolutionary order depends on a continuation of the mass patronage that the revolutionaries acquired before they attained formal political power. To sustain power, they now need to deliver the goods which they promised, or to at least divert attention from them by fomenting popular anger against enemies of the new order, real or imagined. Diverting attention they indeed do, as the many instances of politically sanctioned post-revolutionary violence, wars and other international disputes, and purges and the elimination of "counter-revolutionaries" demonstrate. But even if only symbolic, a token delivery of the goods promised is necessary to maintain the viability of the new system. The result is populist and politically inclusionary regimes, regimes that allow greater participation in the body politic if not in the actual decision making process.

It is here in these inclusionary, post-revolutionary regimes that revolutions meet an embryonic death. Various means of patronage such as economic reforms, programmes for public welfare, and greater political participation, no matter how farcical and cosmetic, heighten the new regime's sense of legitimacy among the population and, at least so long as that legitimacy lasts, immune it from another revolution. Moreover, post-revolutionary regimes, which in any event owe their very genesis to violence, feel less inhibited to use coercion in order to preserve their newly-acquired powers than would otherwise be the case. The constant identification of counter-revolutionary elements as the prime public enemy, the perpetual sense of besiegement and threat from outside forces, and the unending rhetoric of denouncing the morbid past all make post-revolutionary regimes more prone to using violence against actual or perceived sources of opposition. Crushing those who oppose the new order is indeed one of the very sources upon which its legitimacy is based. Interconnected as they often are, new forms of legitimacy and an uninhibited reliance on violence are the most potent preservers post-revolutionary states. At the same time, and largely as a result of these developments, the powers and the structure of the state become much more centralized, leading to a much higher concentration of power in state hands than in pre-revolutionary times (discussed below).

Legitimacy and the Post-Revolutionary State

Much of the efforts of post-revolutionary states can be understood as attempts to find new means of political legitimation. New means of legitimacy may come in various forms, from engagement in international conflicts to attempts to incorporate the masses into the political process and suppress dissenters. On a most fundamental level, the legitimacy of new ruling elites depends on their ability not just to lead revolutions but to deliver on the promises they made during the revolutionary struggle.[51] The economic performance of the post-revolutionary state is thus instrumental in its degree of legitimacy, particularly since the hopes of its participants (who are now its clients) had been raised to a high pitch during the struggle.[52]

In some instances, however, revolutionary movements were neither the result of gross economic disparities within society nor did, as a result, revolutionary figures promise extensive restructuring of economic relations in the new regime. Instead, the wrath of the revolution was directed at those perceived to be governing the country illegitimately and through unauthentic behavior. In these historic examples, the most striking of which occurred in Iran, the values attached to new political institutions and practices, and the manner of conduct of individual actors themselves assume legitimizing functions.[53] Related to this authenticating form of legitimation are a host of symbolic means, such as greater public participation in the political process, in order to bridge the identity gap between the rule and the rulers, and the creation of new political symbols and means of identity

with which the masses could identify.   Often, the memory of
fallen revolutionary heroes is kept alive and used by the regime
as a source of legitimation.[54] All of these mechanisms are
designed to enhance the legitimacy of the new order among the
various social classes, particularly those whose support was
essential in leading to the success of the revolution.

The inclusion of previously politically-disenfranchised
groups into the political process, even if more cosmetic than
substantive, is a major source of legitimacy for post-revolutionary
states. Compared to exclusionary regimes, which are often based
on brittle and inherently weak authoritarian bureaucracies,
inclusionary, populist states enjoy far greater solidity both
insofar as their institutional viability is concerned and in
relation to their popular legitimacy throughout society.
Whereas bureaucratic-authoritarian regimes rely on the
exclusion of the masses from politics, populist ones specifically
aim to establish a mass-based political system. They rely on
collective behavior and on other forms of mass mobilization as
one of their primary supporting pillars. Along with
authoritarian mechanisms, popular mobilization is used as a tool
for state-building.[55] Emphasis is put on the symbolic dimensions
of public affairs, manifested in the form of street marches,
demonstrations, and collective outbursts of political jubilation
and support. Participation enhances the citizen's subjective sense
of governmental legitimacy by the very fact that one feels
involved in the act of governing.[56] Although such ritualistic
ceremonies are often "little more than a cheap means to achieve
political acquiescence," they are intrinsically valuable as they
often bestow on people a sense of self-identity and self-concept.[57]
For the masses who were once excluded from the political process,
participation in events heavily impregnated with political
symbolism results in a sense of enhanced popular involvement in
national political life.[58] Although such regimes may be as
dictatorial as traditional authoritarian bureaucracies, their
incorporation of the masses into the political process makes them
appear as popular democracies. In this sense, populist regimes
enjoy a degree of popular legitimacy unsurpassed by others. It is
this heightened sense of regime legitimacy, brought on by the
ostensibly democratizing effects of mass mobilization, which
enables such regimes to motivate their population to make

supreme sacrifices for the nation.[59]

Revolution and the Politics of Inclusion

Significantly, post-revolutionary polities invariably assume the form of populist, inclusionary regimes. In such political structures, mass mobilization is achieved even before the establishment of new political institutions, and at a time when emotional and ideological bonds linking revolutionary leaders with the masses are strongest. Such links are greatly strengthened with the acquisition of power by the revolutionaries, reinforced by an increasing, mutual reliance by each side on the other. The new leaders need their supporters more than ever before in order to augment their tenuous hold on power, while the masses rely on their leaders to deliver the promised goods for which they endured the traumas of revolution.

What thus emerges out of revolutions is ideologically reconstructed national identities involving the sudden incorporation of formerly excluded popular groups into state-directed projects.[60] Such projects frequently include economic self-help plans, intense efforts aimed at inculcating a new culture and national identity, and, when congenial, international wars. Many post-revolutionary regimes have excelled at channelling popular participation into international wars. Because of the way that revolutionary leaders mobilize popular groups during their struggle for state power, the new regime can tackle mobilization for war better than any other task, including the promotion of economic development. The realization of this potential depends on threatening but not overwhelming geopolitical, international circumstances.[61] By their very nature, post-revolutionary states are more prone to engage in international wars, or at least give off the impression that an attack by a hostile foreign power is imminent. Vilifying international actors as patrons of the state's internal enemies gives post-revolutionary regimes much room for justifying repressive policies and campaigns of terror. At the same time, however, it darkens the diplomatic relations of the post-revolutionary state and those it accuses of collusion with its enemies. The likelihood of engaging in international conflicts is further increased because most post-revolutionary states voice challenges to the diplomatic status quo, seeing prevailing international arrangements as inimical to their new, "radical" priorities. Furthermore, since most of these states have yet to solidify their hold on domestic institutions, they look for support among international allies, some of whom may be advocating revolutions in their own countries, thus leading to overt hostilities between the two respective governments.

Wars are, however, materially and humanly costly ventures and are, as a result, impermanent. Even the longest of the protracted wars in which post-revolutionary regimes engage, such as Iran's war with Iraq in the 1980s, eventually simmer down and turn into bombastic rhetoric. Outlasting wars as politically solidifying agents are ceaseless efforts aimed at redefining popular national identity and the citizens's perceptions of themselves and of their nation. In its ambitious quest to create a new man, the state micro-manages politics. It initiates various plans and projects--through the media, the sponsorship of various acts of collective behavior, and "educational" efforts of varying subtlety--in order to enhance its own legitimacy by minimizing the state-society gap and in the process creating a new political culture suited to its own purposes. As one observer of Cuba's post-revolutionary politics has noted, even the apparently spontaneous demonstrations of support for the regime are staged and carefully coordinated.

> What may appear to the untrained eye as an immense sea of anonymous faces of persons temporarily detached from their customary social relations to participate in the *jurnadas* of the revolutionary calendar is instead a publicly acknowledged, carefully rehearsed, and studied choreographic exercise of groups who are firmly attached to existing institutions and occupy clearly specified and lasting niches.[62]

The conventionalization of collective behavior is a particularly rewarding practice for keeping the elite's ideology alive and maintaining elite-mass linkage. By encouraging mass participation, it separates the devout from nominal followers.

Furthermore, it perpetuates the legitimacy of the regime by keeping the revolutionary spirit alive.[63]

Revolution and National Identity

The cornerstone of the legitimacy of post-revolutionary states is the popular cultivation of a new national identity. The question of what it is to be a citizen of Russia, China, Cuba, Iran, or any other country where a revolution might have occurred assumes a completely different answer after the success of the revolution and the subsequent establishment of the new order. Symbols of collective identity and those with which regimes legitimize themselves, basic cultural orientations and codes of conduct, all assume radically different characters in post-revolutionary states.[64] By incorporating formerly excluded popular groups into state-directed projects, revolutions promote "ideologically restructured national identities."[65] This new identity is one much more at ease with itself, proud of its contribution to the revolutionary struggle, and now, due to its apparent or actual participation in the political process, empowered with a new sense of authority and mission in life. "What revolutionaries offer themselves and their own societies," according to one observer, "is above all else an image of power, control, certainty and purpose in a world in which impotence, incomprehension and terror of sheer meaninglessness are permanent threats."[66] The poor and the politically servile, previously conditioned to a self-acceptance of inferiority and subordinate status, acquire a new sense of power, one of not only being counted but being able to avenge past misfortunes through their newly-found political clout.[67] At least in so far as the symbolic aspects of politics are concerned, the state and society are drawn closer together, the former deliberately forging valuative and emotional bonds with the latter.

Popular legitimacy, or, as the case may be, mass devotion, greatly strengthens the solidity of the central government. An additional element that significantly enhances the powers of post-revolutionary states is their greater willingness to rely on coercion and brute force in order to retain power. Post-revolutionary states, emerging as they often do in the midst of violent inter-elite struggles, wars and other forms of

international conflict, shifting symbols and new national
identities, and the incorporation of the masses into the political
process, are much stronger and politically more centralized in
comparison to the states they replace. This relative strength and
centralization is due not only to the popular support that such
polities cultivate but also a result of the ease with which they
employ coercion in order to stay in power. Reliance on coercion as
a politically sustaining means is especially apparent in states
where the new elites have won power only after a long and
protracted struggle. Success in the violent pursuit and defense of
power habituates leaders to the political use of violence. "Elites
who have secured state power and have maintained their
position by violent means are disposed to respond violently to
future challenges."[68] Revolutions do indeed eat their own
children, with the more powerful victors brutally suppressing
former colleagues for the sake of solidifying their new powers.

Revolution and Purges

Yet the steady elimination of political non-conformists is
part of a broader process of institutionalization, the end result of
which is highly likely to be a police state, at least in the short
run.[69] The bloody and savage purges that invariably follow
every major revolution, from the infamous purges of the Stalin
era to those that followed the Chinese, the Cuban, and the
Iranian revolutions, are more than mere historical coincidences.
They demonstrate a preoccupation on the part of new elites to
secure their powers first against deviating "counter-
revolutionaries" and then against would-be "separatists."[70]
Having relied on violence to acquire their new powers, and in the
process having risked a great deal, revolutionary elites seldom
have any inhibitions about continuing to rely on violence in order
to protect their new privileges.[71] As a result, emerging
post-revolutionary state are often far more brutally coercive
than the ones they replace, suppressing actual or perceived
sources of opposition with considerably less restraint than did
their predecessors. In some instances violence is so endemic--as in
China, for example, where an estimated 100,000 people were
executed in the first half of 1951[72]--that certain forms of
violence are symbolically upheld and even assume a measure of

popular cultural acceptability.[73] The ends, often visions held in high esteem by the new ruling elite, justify the means regardless of how violent and brutal they may be. Terrorist assassinations, firing squads, summary executions, and torture all become socially less vile and more acceptable. After all, insofar as the popular classes see it, those punished by such means *must* be guilty of the highest of crime, that of opposing the new political order.

The Party and the State

Political centralization, endemic violence, and inclusionary institutional arrangements frequently give birth to one-party systems. As earlier discussed, access to organizational means of mobilisation is often crucial in facilitating the hegemony of one group of leaders over others. Thus even in spontaneous revolutions, the seeds of post-revolutionary parties are sown early on. Single, highly centralized political parties are often the most visible institutional manifestations of post-revolutionary states. At least initially in the life of post-revolutionary states, single, official parties play a pivotal role in their institutionalization. This central role is played at two specific levels. Firstly, the political party is designed to augment the organizational reach of the new state at a time when existing state institutions such as the bureaucracy and the military are undergoing purges and being revamped. The party does not so much set policy as it serves as an auxiliary to institutions that have been paralyzed by the weight of the revolution. Its specific intent is to give direction to the new regime's many goals and agendas, goals that are at best onerous and at worst extremely intractable. As such, these parties are "all-encompassing," at once performing a multitude of functions through which the new state's longevity is perpetuated. With the political party in place and at work, the raw, largely uncoordinated energy of mass demonstrators can be channelled in the direction of enhancing the solidity of the new order. Through providing for a means of participation, albeit controlled participation, the party also enhances the new order's legitimacy.[74] By virtue of its ideology, agendas, and organs, it becomes the most popularly inclusive organization of the emerging inclusionary regime. Whereas the other newly-established state mechanisms focus on directing the ideological agendas of new leaders, the political party becomes the primary nexus linking state and society, a nexus which is now all the more important considering the particular relationship of revolutionary leaders to the various social classes. The party becomes the principal venue for political participation. Its cells and affiliated organizations, blessed with official backing and immuned from criticism in the stifling post-revolutionary environment, grow both in their geographic purview and in membership. It thus becomes a pivotal instrument in recruiting leaders at both the intermediate and the top levels of government.[75]

Secondly, the party serves as an instrument of doctrinal and valuative legitimacy for the new power elite. It becomes an instrument of propaganda for the new state, a mean through which the ideology of new political actors is popularized among the social strata. The emphasis on the party as an ideological pillar of the state assumes even greater importance in instances where emerging state institutions remain weak and vulnerable for some time to come, as in non-communist revolutions, when the establishment of new organizations may not have the drive and zeal imbedded in Marxist-Leninist doctrines.[76] In either case, the intertwined nature of single parties and political ideologies are of immense significance in the institutionalisation of post-revolutionary states, communist or not. To begin with, the ideological platform of the party is part of the dominant dogma of the day. Thus membership in the party or even mere participation in its activities entails a significant amount of political socialization. But official, state parties, particularly post-revolutionary ones, resort to a number of far more obvious forms of ideological propaganda. They frequently sponsor lectures and forums for the study and discussion of the dominant ideology. More often they print various publications, from books and essays to newspapers, which are heavily tainted with the ideology of the day. In most post-revolutionary states, the most dominant daily newspapers are those published by the state party. Such newspapers as *Pravda*, China's *Peoples' Daily*, the Cuban *Granma*, and Iran's *Jomhouri Islami* serve functions deeper than formulating state policies.[77] More importantly, at least a t the outset of their publication, they were intended to be further means of political indoctrination.

For the most part, official, post-revolutionary parties are largely discarded once they have outlived their practical and ideological utility. Initially, state parties serve as means of attaining institutionalization through facilitating mobilization, legitimacy, indoctrination, and recruitment. They also serve as surrogates for the bureaucracy at a time of partial or complete bureaucratic paralysis. But once institutionalization is achieved and the new order is on solid organizational and doctrinal grounds, when the bureaucracy is on its feet again and the previously tenuous ideology of the elite has become an unavoidable feature of the establishment, the official state party can potentially pose a threat by becoming a powerful and autonomous base for specific individuals within the elite. This is particularly the case in non-communist states, where official parties are not necessarily embedded in the revolutionary ideology itself but are rather more of a practical tool for furthering the revolution. Once the revolution is achieved and in the eyes of its leaders victorious, there is no longer a need for the organization that had spearheaded it. Once central to the political formulas of the new order, it now becomes a source of nuisance, an organ which did its job well but whose glory is past. Its revolutionary message is misplaced. And its far-reaching and viable organizations are more of a threat than an asset. In so many African states in particular, the parties which valiantly headed wars of national liberation were left to languish once independence was at hand.[78] Many linger in shadow of a glory past, while others become the personal domain of avaricious politicians. Most become empty symbols.[79] In Iran, the once mighty Islamic Republic Party was ordered to disband altogether by Khomeini in 1987.[80]

Factionalism in the Post-Revolutionary State

The fate of official political parties in post-revolutionary regimes is to some extent related to a broader process which such regimes almost invariably undergo, namely factionalism. The appearance of factional groupings within a political system may either be a product of the skewed evolution of post-revolutionary institutions, or, as is often the case in non-revolutionary regimes, a result of purposeful political engineering. A variety of political establishments, particularly those which embody various forms of patrimonial rule, deliberately encourage the existence of different political factions whose competitive efforts against each other are designed to ensure the longevity of the leader at the top.[81]

Even after the eliminatory process of post-revolutionary selection of leaders has run its course and those surviving have been filtered through rigid doctrinal and practical purges, there is still a tendency toward the clustering together of factions within the political establishment, each operating through one of the new institutions of the regime which are just beginning to take form. Individuals emphasising one specific aspect of the dominant ideology may become concentrated in one particular institution--the army, the official party, or a specific ministry, for example--while others with different doctrinal priorities may be clustered in another institution. At times factions form around clashing personalities and egos, when the personal bonds between individuals once prominent in the revolutionary struggle fall victim to brute political realities. Often personal cleavages are reinforced by differing doctrinal interpretations within the broader context of the governing ideology. The persistence of such factional tendencies despite persistent purges in post-revolutionary regimes is due to the very fine subtleties which separate the doctrines of each of the factions. In relatively broad terms, they all adhere to the revolution and its ideals as proclaimed by its current victors. They do, however, seek to pursue specific agendas within the general contours of the post-revolutionary environment, agendas which may or may not find equally enthusiastic supporters among other political leaders. Some of the more common doctrinal issues which frequently lead to factional divisiveness include different views over the prudence or the manner of exporting the revolution abroad, or, more broadly, the implementation of specific, controversial policies, particularly those relating to diplomacy and the economy. The Trotskyite position of exporting the Russian revolution abroad, exemplified in the slogan "World revolution now!", and subsequent factional struggles within the Bolsheviks find parallels in the post-revolutionary governments of China,

Cuba, Iran, and those which follow virtually every other major revolution. [82]

The endemic appearance of factions within post-revolutionary governments is a product of the stunted and tenuous growth of their institutions, at least in the initial phases following their establishment. In a sense, the development of factions among post-revolutionary leaders and the resonance of factional politics in the emerging political machinery is inherent in institutional developments which follow successful revolutions. As earlier discussed, the political arena emerging immediately following the overthrow of the old order is characterized by two, very intense parallel developments: on the one hand the institutions of the *regime* are dying out or being radically restructured while, on the other hand, victorious leaders are jockeying for positions among themselves and are, in the process, eliminating competitors. Thus by nature those institutions that are emerging anew or are being completely revamped assume much greater significance than their functions would ordinarily accord them.

They become, additionally, bases of support for individuals or factions with specific interests, providing them with institutional means of support and organization. Moreover, the inclusionary nature of the regime itself and its efforts at incorporating the masses into the political process enable each faction to use its institutional base to appeal to specific segments of the population. Poor peasants, the proletariat, industrial laborers, civil servants, and soldiers and other army officers are some of the more convenient targets whose support is often sought by specific groups within the new cadre of leaders. Efforts at cultivating such ties take place based on the ideological orientations of the former and the preferences of the latter. Groups favoring more radical economic policies, such as a more extensive redistribution of land or the nationalization of a greater number of private interests, may appeal to those groups for whom economic gains have been the most elusive, the peasants and the poor, the disenfranchised and the wretched. Others, calling for a more vigourous pursuit of the revolution's domestic and foreign enemies, may direct their message at those for whom such threats have a more tangible meaning, groups such as army officers and newly appointed or promoted bureaucrats.

As a result, factionalism is institutionally perpetuated and given strength. Ultimately, the strength of each faction, derived from the viability and importance of the institutions at its disposal and the numerical size and political importance of its target audience, determines the fate of the other factions and the nature of policies pursued by the revolutionary government.

The Difficulties of Transition

Another facet of institutionalization in post-revolutionary regimes involves their inability to devise institutions and procedures designed to ensure a smooth transition of power from present leaders to future successors. This is a problem inherent in socialist systems and, to the extent that the majority of post-revolutionary regimes have been socialist, attention needs to focus on the structural shortcoming of socialist governments regarding the specific issue of leadership succession.[83] Nevertheless, in the non-socialist regimes which emerged out of the French, Mexican, Algerian, and the Iranian revolutions, an orderly and smooth process of leadership succession was also not attained until well into the life of the new political system.[84] In fact, decades well into the life of these post-revolutionary regimes, France and to a lesser extent Mexico remain the only countries in which procedures for a regular turnover of political leaders have been adopted and widely accepted.

Again, an institutionally-induced absence of means for a smooth succession of leaders is rooted in the skewed political evolution of post-revolutionary states. Emphasis is on securing newly-acquired powers and only scant or at best cosmetic attention is paid to mechanisms for power transfer. The political elite are concerned not with devising ways of relinquishing their powers to succeeding leaders but rather with how best to solidify their hold on newly-won privileges. The factional underpinnings of the political environment, coupled with the innate centralized tendencies of post-revolutionary regimes, serve as further impediments to the development and substantive growth of institutional venues for succession.

As a result of these combined factors, post-revolutionary states face their greatest (domestic) challenge when confronted with a need to transfer power from one generation of leaders to the next. At stake is the future course of the revolution. Because the new leaders are rarely predetermined, because there are factions within the leadership with subtle but pronounced ideological agendas, and because a consensual process for the election of new leaders is conspicuously absent, then with the change of leaders the revolutionary state may take a dramatic turn in direction, as it did with the passing of successive Soviet leaders, as occurred in China with the death of Chairman Mao, in Iran with the death of Khomeini, and may well occur in Cuba after Castro's departure. Only in Nicaragua's post-revolutionary state, where international dynamics played a far greater and more direct role than perhaps in any other post-revolutionary state, were there elections designed to determine the second generation leaders of the new regime.

ECONOMY

In their efforts to attain full institutionalization and at the same time perpetuate their popular legitimacy, post-revolutionary regimes are forced to pay close and detailed attention to economy. Most revolutionary movements, in fact, particularly planned ones, base much of their legitimacy on promises of redistributing wealth and reformulating economic relationships once they acquire power. Whereas some revolutions may be "authenticating" in the sense of emphasising the legitimacy of new symbols and new forms of identity, many other revolutionary movements put greater emphasis on the need for a redistribution of economic goods among the popular classes.[85] By nature, such revolutionary movements and the post-revolutionary regimes to which they subsequently give birth are strongly committed to carrying out redistributive economic policies.

Yet despite the varying degrees of emphasis on symbols as opposed to more tangible economic considerations by leaders of different revolutionary movements, all post-revolutionary states have much at stake in ensuring the economic well-being of their new constituents. For such regimes, much of their viability and support depends on their ability to make good on the promises of the revolution, on ensuring that their followers's actual economic status improves and that they no longer feel completely disenfranchised from society. Particularly in planned revolutions, where the banner of revolution is raised in the name of particular social classes--often the peasantry, as most Latin American examples demonstrate[86]--the bulk of the post-revolutionary project is devoted to enhancing the economic positions of those classes. Traditional oligarchies are replaced through a "continuous process of replacement and restructuring of elites,"[87] with the new elites (at least in rhetoric if not in substance) being the previously disenfranchised. Thus regardless of their dogma and zealous rhetoric, the seemingly dramatic economic restructuring efforts of most post-revolutionary regimes are as much products of immediate political necessities as they are a result pre-determined of doctrinal agendas.

Land Reform and Nationalization

Efforts by post-revolutionary regimes aimed at achieving economic reforms and restructuring often manifest themselves in the form of confiscations of land, assets, and other pieces of property, nationalization of industries, and the introduction of mechanisms designed to control the flow and concentration of capital. The confiscation and redistribution of land from proprietors to peasants and serfs is by far the most dramatic and vivid manifestation of economic transformation under post-revolutionary regimes. In a sense, the intensely emotional nature of the whole drama and its resulting societal dislocations--land being confiscated from heartless and brutal feudal lords and given to miserable peasants--cause post-revolutionary land reform programs to be carried out with much fanfare and make considerable noise both at home and abroad. At the same time, the process of land reform is itself at once economically, politically, socially, culturally, and psychologically transforming and, at times, violent.[88] It creates a solid link between the state and a segment of society whose support is now central to the new political formula. With the old elite physically eliminated or at least economically immobilized, those previously left out of the economic mainstream--peasants and the proletariat, laborers and industrial workers--are made to feel that they are now the elite, the state directing its boisterous economic propaganda toward them instead of the capitalists and industrial magnates, feudal lords and aristocratic families.

But even in instances where land reform is carried out half-heartedly or is aborted soon after a noisy start, post-revolutionary regimes invariably attempt to redirect the flow of income and capital away from certain classes and toward others. The principal means of such efforts at economic redistribution are the institution of regulative policies and widespread nationlization, with the government retaining control over the confiscated assets on behalf of the larger society.[89] The primary targets of nationalization are often those economic concerns through which wealth in the *regime* was accumulated in the most conspicuous manner, wealth which was in turn flaunted by the regime's select class of economic beneficiaries. Large factories and successful firms, privately owned banks and insurance agencies, import-export businesses and larger stores, all are among the first wave of economic concerns to become nationalized by post-revolutionary regimes.

Often specific agencies are set up by the government to coordinate the redistributive economic agendas of the new regime or to manage and run the new state-owned companies. State cooperatives are established in order to overlook the production and sale of agricultural and other consumer goods. Large private enterprises are turned into parastatals and become an integral part of the new regime's economic plan. Through these and other initiatives, post-revolutionary regimes often try to penetrate into deeper levels of economic activity and, consequently, enhance their politically centralized structures to an even greater degree by assuming an increasing array of economic responsibilities.

Great Expectations, Declining Abilities

Ironically, attempts to enhance the living standards of a substantial portion of the population and to concurrently augment the economic purviews of the post-revolutionary state take place within a context of declining state abilities and mounting economic difficulties. Because of the very redistributive goals that post-revolutionary regimes set for themselves, coupled with the limited and often depleted base of resources they have at their disposal, post-revolutionary regimes invariably face a compendium of economic problems, exacerbating the difficulties, particularly in the short run, as they attempt to remedy them.

Such economic quandaries are to a large extent inherent to the nature of post-revolutionary regimes, although they are also accented by the overall tumults and traumas of revolution. To begin with, the state's efforts aimed at achieving greater dominance in the economic sphere lead to apprehensions and uncertainties in the private sector and foster a general tendency to pull capital and investments out of the market for fear of partial confiscation or outright nationalization. At the same time, managerial and restructuring changes in the newly-nationalized enterprises lead to declining productivity and dwindling surpluses.[90] The negative economic ramifications of such an environment are aggravated by policies pursued by post-revolutionary regimes themselves. At a time when economic realities necessitate a fall in living standards, official attempts are made to enhance the people's economic largess. Often large increases in money wages are allocated, the consumption of food and other basic goods are subsidized, and social security nets are expanded. However, while these and other similar policies designed to aid impoverished sectors absorb large amounts of resources, they do very little to raise the level of economic output and in fact merely stretch the state's meager resources even thinner. The targets of the state's economic efforts, namely the poor and the disenfranchised, are marginal to the rest of the economy and do not directly contribute to its growth and improvement. Those economically active sectors that are important to the overall health of the economy, meanwhile, the producers and industrialists, merchants and investors, see themselves constantly threatened by the possibility of nationalization or, at best, by state harassments designed to win over the support and sympathy of consumers.[91]

Combined, these policies and the broader context within which they are formulated often lead to serious economic crises or, at best, exigencies of one kind or another. Invariably, post-revolutionary polities encounter significant difficulties in the economic domain. Increased concern over the repercussions of poor economic performance often result in the allocation of resources in ways inconsistent with revolutionary rhetoric. The need to maintain production prompts post-revolutionary regimes to allocate state resources where they can be most productive.[92] Certain policies may also be devised and implemented based not on their revolutionary merits but on their attractiveness to foreign, primarily Western, creditors and banking agencies. Moreover, due to the tenuous nature of political institutions in initial phases of the revolution, many of the regime's far-reaching economic reform projects lack the necessary political muscle needed to ensure their full and unimpeded implementation.

However, various forms of agrarian reform and land redistribution plans, often among the most pressing goals of post-revolutionary regimes, are carried out at best only partially and face challenges from numerous entrenched interests. If not aborted due to the outright interference of entrenched landed interests, agrarian reforms often fall prey to inconspicuous government fiscal and monitory policies.[93] At best, the sharp edges of such reform plans are frequently muted under the weight of bureaucratic procedures and mountains of paperwork. These largely abortive measures are likely to compound rather than alleviate the economic miseries facing peasants and other underprivileged classes.

However, mass incorporation into the political process under the auspices of inclusionary populism, coupled with the launching of welfare policies, perpetuates a perceived sense of political and even economic betterment on the part such disenfranchised groups. Such fallacious perceptions of economic progress do not, however, in any sense entangle the middle classes, whose real and perceived economic positions decline rather starkly as compared to pre-revolutionary times. For the most part, the middle classes are in the employ of the state, particularly in the bureaucracy. Forming one of the most important sources of support for most pre-revolutionary regimes (along with the armed forces), bureaucracies are subject to the most exhaustive purges following revolutions and at the same time experience the greatest degree of paralysis as a result of revolutionary upheavals. Efforts designed to curb corruption and inefficiency in state institutions, themselves among the rallying cries of the revolution, further erode the once intractable powers of the bureaucracy. In simple economic terms, the principal source of income for the middle class, namely the state bureaucracy, undergoes considerable stress and flux immediately following revolutions and, as a result, the economic purchase of the middle class is proportionately reduced.

By and large, the economies of post-revolutionary regimes need to be examined within the context of embryonic processes of political institutionalization, inclusionary political arrangements, and the contradictory forces of supply and demand in relation to the state's capacities and its aspirations. Regimes emerging out of successful planned revolutions, which by nature embody previously devised economic platforms, have far more pointed economic agendas compared to other post-revolutionary regimes, at least initially, because they made specific promises to specific groups during the revolution and are now having to materialize them. Much of their legitimacy and continued support now depends on their ability to make good on the economic promises made during the revolutionary struggle. That is largely why extensive efforts at land reform were launched following the Chinese, Cuban, and the Nicaraguan revolutions, during each of which peasant support was sought through promises of economic betterment and redistribution of land. Yet the pressing need to maintain popular support prompts regimes emerging out of spontaneous revolutions to also pay close attention to the economy and attempt to better the lives of previously disenfranchised popular classes. Despite laudable intentions and extensive measures designed to restructure economic relations and redistribute available resources, however, the structural limitation that entangle post-revolutionary regimes invariably lead to economic slowdowns and at times even serious crises. Attempts to address such politically troublesome economic shortcomings, often coupled with stringent conditions set by international patrons or creditors, frequently lead to a mutation of the economic agendas of post-revolutionary regimes and a gradual return of less restrictive regulatory policies.

CONCLUSION

By definition, revolutions give birth to political systems radically different from the ones they replaced. New symbols and values, new forms of identity and modes of conduct, and new organizations and institutions emerge and replace those of the Old Order. In short, revolutions lead to changes in both the subjective as well as the objective aspects of political life. Within this context, the most noticeable change in the political character of post-revolutionary regimes occurs in the composition of their leaders. The stewards of post-revolutionary regimes are determined not necessarily by virtue of their revolutionary credentials, political wiliness, or charisma--although these are often crucial auxiliary factors--but primarily by the extent and viability of institutions at their disposal which could form effective links between them and the larger society. At a time when existing, political and non-political institutions of the Old Order have fallen under the weight of revolution, when society is left with at best tenuous forms of political leadership, the factors which determine the ultimate composition of new and emerging political elites are invariably *institutional* in nature rather than dependent on such extra-institutional dynamics as charisma and political acumen.

In the politically amorphous atmosphere which immediately follows revolutions, what counts are the various links and nexes which bind new political aspirants to those segments of the population whose political input matters. In planned revolutions, these mobilizational links are invariably established through the very organization which defeated the government and established itself as its rightful successor, namely the revolutionary guerrilla party. Once the forces of the Old Order are defeated and its organizations paralyzed, the only viable institution which can penetrate society and lay claim to its political mantel is the party organization which spearheaded the revolution and overwhelmed the forces of the government. In fact, the party's very revolutionary victory attests to the viability of its links with the popular classes, links whose purpose becomes one of channelling destructive revolutionary energies into politically constructive goals. Spontaneous revolutions, in contrast, initially lack existing institutional linkages between emerging leaders and the larger society. Compared to planned revolutions, these organisational links between the new elites and the masses emerge somewhat later in spontaneous revolutions. Frequently, new political institutions, often in the form of organized parties, are quickly formed with the aim of institutionalizing the newly-won clout of segments or individuals within the band of revolutionary leaders. The new institutions of the regime itself--its military, legislature, or bureaucracy for example--may also be turned into *de facto* centers of power and influence for specific individuals or factions hoping to enhance their own purchase in the post-revolutionary period.

Significantly, changes which result form revolutionary transformations extend far beyond the mere format and functions of political arrangements. The very nature of emergent post-revolutionary institutions differ. They are inherently much stronger and more centralized, are less hesitant to rely on violence as means of political sustenance, and are married to the society in much more direct ways than pre-revolutionary states. They are, concurrently, transformative in nature, driven by goals of inculcating new symbols and forms of identity among the masses, altering established patterns of social and political behavior, and giving substance to the economic promises of the revolution. Again, these extra-institutional facets of post-revolutionary states manifest themselves both subjectively as well as objectively across the social and political realms. Post-revolutionary centralization and strength are not only political truisms but also translate themselves into the society's image of itself. No longer is the society disillusioned and uncertain of itself the way it was prior to the revolution. It now has a political mandate, backed by moral conviction and zeal.[94] It is a society, in a sense, which feels much more powerful than it did before.[95] Violence, another universal of post-revolutionary states, is also morally and ethically upheld, its distinction as an end unto itself rather than a mean to higher goals becoming increasingly blurred. Moreover, the post-revolutionary fusion of state and society extends beyond institutional links which bind the two together. The incorporation of the society, or at least significant portions of it, into the political process involves as much symbolism and emotional attachment on the part of the former to the latter as it does the creation of inclusionary structures. An entirely new frame of political culture is devised, involving new patterns of political practice, new norms and values, new actors and participants, and a new context within which the whole drama is played out. In short, the world of politics is revolutionized--the old cursed and discarded, the new hailed and upheld.

"Revolutions will come and revolutions will go, but I will continue with mine," said the defiant Mexican revolutionary hero Emiliano Zapata as he flaunted Mexico's post-revolutionary government.[96] There comes a point in the life of every post-revolutionary polity when it needs to realize that it is no longer *revolutionary*, that it needs to get on with the conduct of politics free of rhetoric and zeal, albeit still under different auspices. Zapata's refusal to let go of the Mexican revolution was as much symptomatic of an instinctive need by revolutionary leaders for the continuance of their cause as it was a result of the frustration of his hopes for agrarian reforms.[97] In the same way that wars never end for warriors, revolutions never end for revolutionaries. But the popular fervor of revolution is inherently impermanent, bound to eventually subside because of its very intensity and scale. Street demonstrations, marches, slogans, and bombastic rhetoric may be good for the upkeep of symbols, but they don't necessarily enhance the people's economic lot. Everyday life has to somehow return to normal; society cannot run on a permanent revolutionary footing.

Accentuating this need for a return to social and political normalcy is the inevitable waning of charismatic authority and the need to eventually replace it with regularized procedures and institutionalized forms of power. The invisible bonds that glue the masses to their revolutionary heros need to be transformed into actual political institutions, be they new political parties and organizations or pre-existing institutions manipulated accordingly. To maintain that revolutions die is to overlook their lingering legacies as manifested in the institutions, political cultures, and patterns of practice to which they give birth. These new characteristics permeate every aspect of post-revolutionary states, and, by all indications, never completely cease to a part of them. But they become routine, losing their zeal and ferocity over time. Successful revolutions do not die; they first give birth to post-revolutionary states and then slowly subside.

Notes

1. For two differing historical interpretations on the termination of the Russian revolution see Lionel Kochan, *Russia in Revolution, 1890-1918* (London: Granada, 1966), and Sheila Fitzpatrick, *The Russian Revolution, 1917-1932* (Oxford: Oxford University Press, 1982).

2. For comprehensive historical accounts of the Russian, Mexican, Chinese, Yugoslav, Vietnamese, Algerian, Turkish, and Cuban revolutions, see John Dunn, *Modern Revolutions: Introduction to a Political Phenomenon* (Cambridge: Cambridge University Press, 1972). For a discussion of the Iranian revolution, see Mehran Kamrava, *The Political History of Modern Iran: From Tribalism to Theocracy* (New York: Praeger, 1992).

3. The refusal of revolutionary leaders to accept the eventual petering out of the revolutionary movement is demonstrated through their unrelenting rhetoric while in office. Similarly, they frequently engage in activities or launch initiatives which may appear illogical by conventional norms. Their rhetoric and seemingly unreasonable efforts are all part of the process of institutionalization, designed to maximize their own longevity by prolonging the fervor of the revolution and at the same time re-directing it into politically advantageous energies.

4. Theda Skocpol, *States and Social Revolutions* (Cambridge: Cambridge University Press, 1979), p. 163.

5. Ibid, pp. 163-4.

6. See above, Chap. 2.

7. See Dunn, *Modern Revolutions*.

8. Crane Brinton, *The Anatomy of Revolution* (New York: Prentice-Hall, 1952), p. 134.

9. Ibid, p. 226.

10. Ibid, p. 136.

11. Ibid, pp. 158-9.

12. Ibid, p. 163.

13. Ibid, p. 179.

14. Ibid, pp. 163-4.

15. Ibid, p. 224.

16. Ibid, p. 229.

17. Ibid.

18. Skocpol, *States and Social Revolutions*, p. 171.

19. Ibid.

20. Ibid, p. 280.

21. Ibid, p. 284.

22. S.N. Eisenstadt, *Revolution and the Transformation of Societies* (New York: Free Press, 1978), p. 251. Eisenstadt also draws attention to the "major institutional derivatives of the symbolic orientations and their institutional derivatives such as, of human activities or the ground rules of social interaction, the structure of centers, center-periphery relations, the structure of markets, and so on. (Also important are,) among the principle actors in the revolutionary processes, the major carriers of such orientations; that is, the institutional entrepreneurs and elites that shape the institutional contours through which seemingly similar institutional interests are modeled in different ways." Ibid, p. 222.

23. Theda Skocpol, "Rentier State and Shi'a Islam in the Iranian Revolution," *Theory and Society* vol. 11, no. 3 (May 1982), p. 277. The reference to modernity in this passage has to do with the author's discussion of the social background of the Iranian revolution, prior to which extensive social and economic changes occurred.

24. Ibid, pp. 275-6.

25. Brinton, *Anatomy of Revolution*.

26. For critical examinations of Skocpol's analysis see the articles by Nikki Keddie, Eqbal Ahmad, and Walter Goldfrank in *Theory and Society* vol. 11, no. 3, pp. 285-303, and Jerome Himmelstein and Michael Kimmel, "Review Essay: States and Social Revolutions: The Implications and Limits of Skocpol's Structural Model," *American Journal of Sociology* vol. 86, no. 5 (1981), pp. 1145-54.

27. See Eisenstadt, *Revolutions and the Transformation of Societies*, pp. 223-51.

28. See Brinton,*The Anatomy of Revolution*, Chaps. 4 and 5, and Eisenstadt, *Revolution and the Transformation of Societies*, pp. 222-3.

29. Skocpol, *States and Social Revolutions*, p. 165.

30. Ibid, p. 165.

31. Skocpol, "Rentier State and Shi'a Islam in the Iranian Revolution," p. 277.

32. R. Ben Jones, *The French Revolution* (London: Hodder & Stoughton, 1967), pp. 99-100. The *sans-culottes* were a group that fell "midway between what could be called working class and the petty bourgeoisie . . . . They were distinguished by their dress: trousers were worn by the workers, not the knee-breechers (*culottes*) of their richer lawyers . . . . It was a symbol of their egalitarian outlook, for they were resentful of 'rank-pulling.' They were distinguished by a social antagonism, too, for they regarded themselves as virtuous poor and the wealthy as likely to be corrupt and 'aristocratic' (a word which for them came to represent anyone against the revolution)." Ibid, pp. 27-8.

33. Ibid, p. 105.

34. Ibid, p. 121.

35. John Dunn, *Modern Revolutions*, p. 40.

36. Ibid, pp. 42-3.

37. See Shaul Bakhash,*The Reign of the Ayatollahs: Iran and the Islamic Revolution* (London: I. B. Tauris), pp. 56-64.

38. Ibid, p. 31.

39. James DeFronzo, *Revolutions and Revolutionary Movements* (Boulder, CO: Westview, 1991), p. 204. FSLN stands for *Frente Sandanista de Liberacion Nacional*.

40. Brinton, *The Anatomy of Revolution*, p. 135.

41. For a discussion of the intellectual tendencies in the French revolution, namely the *philosophes* and the *physiocrats*, see Jones, *The French Revolution*, pp. 11-17, 63-66.

42. Ernest Gellner. *Plough, Sword and Book: The Structure of Human History* (Chicago: University of Chicago Press, 1988), p. 147.

43. Brinton, *The Anatomy of Revolution*, p. 136.

44. Eisenstadt, *Revolutions and the Transformation of Society*, p. 217.

45. Peter Calvert, *Politics, Power and Revolution: An Introduction to Comparative Politics* (London: Wheatsheaf, 1983), p. 165.

46. Max Weber, *On Charisma and Institution Building* (Chicago: University of Chicago Press, 1968), p. 54.

47. Barry Schultz and Robert Slater, "A Framework for Analysis," Barry Schultz and Robert Slater, eds., *Revolution and Political Change in the Third World* (Boulder, CO: Lynne Rienner, 1990), p. 9.

48. For Russia see John Dunn, *Modern Revolutions*, pp. 24-47. For a discussion of the Cuban Communist Party, see John Griffiths, "The Cuban Communist Party," Vicky Randall, ed., *Political Parties in the Third World* (London: Sage, 1988), pp. 153-73; and for the Islamic Republic Party in Iran, see Mehran Kamrava, *Political History of Modern Iran*, Chapter 4.

49. Barry Rubin, *Modern Dictators: Third World Coup Makers, Strongmen, and Populist Tyrants* (New York: McGraw Hill, 1987), p. 283.

50. For a discussion of "inclusionary regimes," see Mehran Kamrava, *Politics and Society in the Third World* (London: Routledge, 1992).

51. Dunn, *Modern Revolutions*, p. 15.

52. Colburn, *Post-Revolutionary Nicaragua: State, Class, and the Dilemmas of Agrarian Policy* (Berkeley, CA: University of California Press, 1986), p. 22.

53. Manus Midlarsky, "Scarcity and Inequality: Prologue to the Onset of Mass Revolution," *Journal of Conflict Resolution* vol. 26, no. 1,

(March 1982), p. 22.

54. Henri Claessen, "Changing Legitimacy," Ronald Cohen and Judith Toland, eds., *State Formation and Political Legitimacy* (New Brunswick, NJ: Transaction Books, 1988), pp. 36-7.

55. Theda Skocpol, "Social Revolutions and Mass Military Mobilization," *World Politics* vol. XL, no. 2 (January 1988), p. 149.

56. Jan Leighley. "Participation as a Stimulus for Political Conceptualization," *The Journal of Politics* vol. 53, no. 1 (February 1991), p. 198.

57. E.B. Portis, "Charismatic Leadership and Cultural Democracy," *Review of Politics* vol. 41, no. 2 (Spring 1987), pp. 237-8.

58. Skocpol, "Social Revolutions and Mass Military Mobilization," p. 149.

59. Ibid, p. 150.

60. Ibid, p. 164.

61. Ibid, pp. 167-8.

62. B.E. Aguirre, "The Conventionalization of Collective Behavior in Cuba," *American Journal of Sociology* vol. 21, no. 1 (1984), p. 589.

63. Ibid, p. 563.

64. Eisenstadt, *Revolution and the Transformation of Society*, p. 218.

65. Skocpol, "Social Revolutions and Mass Military Mobilization," p. 164.

66. Dunn, *Modern Revolutions*, p. 256.

67. DeFronzo, *Revolutions and Revolutionary Movements*, p. 86.

68. Gurr, "War, Revolution, and the Growth of the Coercive State," *Comparative Politics* vol. 21, no. 1 (April 1988), p. 49.

69. Ibid, p. 53.

70. Rubin, *Modern Dictators*, p. 19.

71. Gurr, "War, Revolution, and the Growth of the Coercive State," p. 53.

72. DeFronzo, *Revolutions and Revolutionary Movements*, p. 85.

73. Eisenstadt, *Revolution and the Transformation of Societies*, p. 218.

74. Clement Moore, "The Single Party as a Source of Legitimacy," Samuel Huntington and Clement Moore, eds., *Authoritarian Politics in Modern Society* (London: Basic Books, 1970), p. 50.

75. Ibid, p. 51.

76. Samuel Huntington, "Social and Institutional Dynamics of One-Party Systems," Huntington and Moore, eds., *Authoritarian Politics in Modern Society* pp. 27-8.

77. For a discussion of these and other communist parties, see Richard Staar, ed., *1991 Yearbook on International Communist Affairs:*

Parties and Revolutionary Movements (Stanford, CA: Hoover Institution Press, 1991).

78. Vicky Randall, "Introduction," Vicky Randall, ed., *Political Parties in the Third World* (London: Sage, 1988), pp. 2-3.

79. Rubin, *Modern Dictators*, p. 312.

80. For more on the Islamic Republican Party and reasons for its dissolution, see Mehran Kamrava, *From Tribalism to Theocracy:*, pp.

81. For a detailed and insightful discussion of patrimonial political arrangements, see Bill and Springborg, *Politics in the Middle East* (Glenview, IL: Scott, Foresman/Little, Brown, 1990), Chap. 4, especially pp. 154-5.

82. For a discussion of tendencies within the post-revolutionary Russian government to export the revolution, see James DeFronzo, *Revolutions and Revolutionary Movements*, pp. 46-7; in the case of China see, Frederick Teiwes, *Politics at Mao's Court: Gao Gang and Party Factionalism in the Early 1950s* (Armonk, NY: M.E. Sharp, 1990); and for Iran's post-revolutionary regime, see Kamrava, *From Tribalism to Theocracy*, Chapter 4.

83. Carl Beck, "Patterns and Problems of Governance," Carmelo Mesa-Lago and Carl Beck, eds., *Comparative Socialist Systems: Essays on Politics and Economics* (Pittsburgh, PA: University Center for International Studies, 1975), p. 136.

84. For the French example, see Skocpol, *States and Social Revolutions*, pp. 182-3; for Iran see Kamrava, *From Tribalism to Theocracy*, Chapter 4.

85. Manus Midlarsky, "Scarcity and Inequality," p. 22.

86. See Robert Dix, "The Varieties of Revolution," *Comparative Politics* vol. 15, no. 3 (April 1983), pp. 281-294, especially 283-7.

87. Eisenstadt, *Revolution and the Transformation of Societies*, p. 279.

88. DeFronzo, *Revolutions and Revolutionary Movements*, p. 86.

89. Colburn, *Post-Revolutionary Nicaragua*, p. 13.

90. Ibid, p. 15.

91. Ibid, pp. 16-18.

92. Ibid, p. 19.

93. Ibid, p. 21.

94. Rubin, *Modern Dictators*, p. 19.

95. Dunn, *Modern Revolutions*, p. 256.

96. Ibid, p. 62.

97. See ibid, pp. 52-66.

4

The Post-Revolutionary Polity

Revolutions, as discussed in earlier chapters, transform not just the actors and institutions of political systems but also symbolic sources of political legitimacy as well as social norms and mores which justify the coming to fore of new political forms. In essence, the legitimacy of the revolutionary state rests on the society's attitudes and perceptions at a much more fundamental level than would otherwise be the case. States cannot operate in a social vacuum and, even if exclusionary in character, are invariably linked to society in one way or another. Whether through sheer coercion or a facade of legitimacy, even the most narrowly-based regimes need somehow to retain ties with specific segments within the larger society in order to both survive and remain functionally viable. The inclusive nature of post-revolutionary states, and their need to provide for systemic means of mass-based political input, significantly increases the importance of the state on the one hand and social actors on the other.

Moreover, precisely because both the state and society have become *revolutionized*, and the underlying rules which govern their respective conducts have subsequently been changed, the nexus between the two assumes particular characteristics. Chapter three examined the states that emerge following revolutions and their influence on society. The present chapter turns the focus of attention on society, analysing those trends and dynamics within post-revolutionary societies which give the entire polity--not just the state but non-state actors as well--the peculiar characteristics which they acquire after revolutions.[1] Having been through an event as traumatic as a revolution, do post-revolutionary societies in fact embody features which in one way or another influence the body politic? If that is indeed the case, it is then important to examine the nature of the interaction between a revolutionary society and a revolutionary state. It is to these questions which this chapter turns.

POST-REVOLUTIONARY SOCIETIES

A revolution is a movement from within society to capture the political power exerted by the state. As such, the launching of a revolutionary movement, and particularly its success, involves considerable adjustments and disturbances on the part of society. Whether the product of collective efforts by large cross sections of society, as in spontaneous revolutions, or the result of initiatives by specific groups, as is the case in planned revolutions, the revolution is brought on and won through the efforts of groups from within society. Apart from the much more intricate and detailed nexes that link the emerging revolutionary states and societies together, post-revolutionary societies acquire additional features which they would not have had had they not experienced a revolution. The revolutionary movement, in a sense, gives rise to specific characteristics within post-revolutionary societies.

At the most fundamental level, such societies are characterized by a lack of social control, a product both of the political incapacitation of the regime, and magnified and intense revolutionary social change. Political activity takes place within a context of changing social and political symbols, the very perceptions that society has of the state having greatly changed. Increased political participation aimed at capturing state institutions in turn polarizes diverging social and political tendencies, while at the same time enhancing the power of independent conceptualization. Efforts aimed at wresting political power away from the regime, meanwhile, result in the development of a host of norms and values supporting political struggle. Specifically, a heightened sense of nationalism and a symbolic upholding of the value of martyrdom become strikingly prevalent, particularly among those social groups who were at the forefront of the political struggle. The society, in essence, becomes just as revolutionized as the state.

On the most general level, revolutions result in changes in the ground rules of social interactions and, subsequently, in the structural and organizational derivatives of these ground rules.[2] Cultural orientations, mores, and norms change, particularly those which relate to political activity, with new symbols replacing the old. A new political culture emerges, and is in turn cultivated by the regime, with mass-based political activism as its core value. Political input is on the one hand encouraged by the emerging inclusionary state and, on the other hand, desired by masses unwilling to forfeit their newly-found political liberties.

Yet despite the appearance of complementarity, the mutual desire of both state and society for popular political input has the potential of engendering conflict. For while the inclusionary state aims at encouraging *controlled* forms of participation, not all social actors desire to partake in guided displays of political expression. The internal conflicts among competing heirs to the revolution which characterize post-revolutionary states in their initial phases of establishment in turn resonate to a conflict of the same nature between social actors and the state. Since revolutions lead to a temporary collapse of the repressive capacities of the government, they invariably result in a period of non-existent or at best minimal social control.[3] Society has become liberated, not just politically but culturally as well. It is embroiled in a process of formulating new values and symbols, new patterns of conduct and new expectations.[4] But the eventual victors of the revolutionary struggle, those who can subdue their previous colleagues and hegemonize the post-revolutionary state, are willing to support such new cultural symbols and values only insofar as they suit their immediate political ends.

In fact, post-revolutionary societies are often marred by coercive and brutal attempts on the part of new elites to establish social control. With a zeal and determination uncharacteristic of past regimes, new elites seek to inculcate among the populace those values and norms which they consider to be the correct ones. These new values form the basis of their legitimacy, and their popular acceptance is central to the success of the new regime.

Value Conflict

The inherently conflictual nature of the relationship between post-revolutionary states and societies does not, at least initially, necessarily translate into political violence. What occurs is more a clash of values, a conflict between values designed to legitimize specific political forms on the one hand and those expressed in rebellion against previously dominant cultural frames of reference on the other. The overt violence which plagues post-revolutionary states is often a product of internal squabbles among various political elites. Nevertheless, culturally-induced political violence in post-revolutionary settings is a possibility.[5] Post-revolutionary states, for whom coercion is frequently synonymous with the process of institutionalization, often do not hesitate to subjugate non-conformist social strata and to ridicule and suppress their values and cultural orientations. In their attempt to "enforce a life without the ordinary vices within a fairly short time,"[6] post-revolutionary governments resort to more than mere invasion of their citizens' privacy.

Their puritanical asceticism is often enforced under the auspices of emerging institutions that are, initially at least, inherently reliant on coercion for their very survival. At the same time, most of the non-conformists, who are by nature more politically aware and opinionated, are reluctant to voluntarily surrender their newly-found social and cultural liberties, having in the meanwhile mustered up the courage of determined political opposition. At least insofar as that segment of the post-revolutionary society is concerned, the preservation of new cultural forms may be viewed as worth fighting for. It is a fight, however, in which the state invariably prevails, its brutal determination to hold on to power and to glorify only those values which it sees as politically prudent proving too cumbersome for cultural hopefuls.

The Repression of Non-Conformists

The quest for political correctness, compellingly pursued by post-revolutionary states, translates into rigid social agendas within which, it is presumed by the governments involved, the legitimacy of the new order is embedded. The reigns of terror that follow revolutions are not just dark political experiences; they are as much projects designed to mold or to at least contain perceived social and cultural non-conformists. Calls for cultural vigilance become part and parcel of post-revolutionary life. Attempts at creating a New Man, socialist or otherwise depending on the revolutionary dictum, become as much socially and culturally intrusive as they are politically stifling. Stalin's Cultural Revolution was designed to eradicate "enemies of the people," Mao's directed against "class enemies." And Khomeini's so-called Hanging Judge strove to stamp out "corruption on Earth."[7]

While the attainment of political consolidation may be central to such projects, their penetrative social and cultural affects cannot be overlooked. But post-revolutionary societies succumb to the cultural edicts of their new rulers only grudgingly at best, the threat of being branded "counter-revolutionary" hanging over the heads of all non-conformists. Yet outbursts of defiance and overt opposition do exist. The violence which accompanied the imposition of moral codes by Iran's victorious revolutionaries is a striking illustration of culturally-based frictions which entangle post-revolutionary polities.[8] The forced imposition of the veil (the *chador*) by Iran's post-revolutionary government, for example, was part of a more comprehensive program designed to ensure the moral purity of the citizenry.[9] But it encountered vociferous opposition from large numbers of Iranian women, for whom the action contradicted everything that the liberating promises of the revolution stood for.[10]

Social Polarization

The tensions which accompany the inculcation of a new cultural frame of reference are compounded by characteristics which post-revolutionary societies themselves assume as a result of the revolutionary experience. Specifically, the divisions which invariably characterize all societies become polarised as a result of the revolutionary experience. While there are no definitive links between *ordinary* forms of political participation (such as voting or membership in parties) and factional polarization,[11] polarization does occur within a context of revolutionary participation. Due to the tumults and intensity of the revolutionary struggle, social, political, and ideological cleavages become polarized, each faction or camp more determined not only to survive in the hostile post-revolutionary atmosphere but also to legitimize itself as the rightful heir of the revolution. Frictions and subtle maneuvers, carried out with a sense of gentility for the sake of a semblance of post-revolutionary unity, soon give way to conflicts which increasingly assume something of a sectarian character.

As the revolution progresses, the stakes become higher. What were once faint and muted differences--be they ethnic, social, cultural, political, or religious in origin--become increasingly cohesive, mutually exclusive tendencies, each being hardened as it undergoes (and to a certain extent carries forward) the revolutionary process. Unspoken pacts and implicit arrangements which previously kept disparate social, ethnic, and economic groups in seeming harmony break up and often degenerate into open warfare, the political glue which once kept them together having come apart.

Polarization occurs at two particular levels. On a general level, the advent and course of the revolutionary movement politicizes the population and, even after a post-revolutionary state has been firmly established, intensifies political beliefs and orientations. But polarization occurs on a more fundamental level also, involving the various tendencies which differentiate the various cultural orientations of post-revolutionary societies. Often after much disquiet, the ensuing political chaos is finally subdued as the New Order consolidates itself. But because social and cultural values are deeply held and concern people's private attitudes and thoughts, it takes longer for new, dominant cultural forms to emerge, and even longer for them to take hold. Social mosaics break apart, not to be reconstructed until well after new leaders can enforce their own cultural hegemony. People with differing orientations vie for greater cultural hegemony, attempting to mold the emerging norms of the New Society according to their own orientations and perceptions. Apart from the new political direction which post-revolutionary states try to lead their societies in, there is an attempt from within post-revolutionary societies to rethink cultural priorities, reformulate dominant values, and redirect social energies. At the least, there are efforts by distinct social groups and segments to superimpose their own cultural values and perceptions on the larger society.

A polarization of social and cultural differences occurs concurrent with, and mutually reinforces, a dramatic rise in the overall level of political awareness and activity by the general population. Revolutionary mobilization, polarity of cultural values, and inclusionary political practices, all of which combine to give post-revolutionary polities an intensely charged character, lead to the "politicization of traditionally non-political social sectors."[12] This politicization is achieved not only through the attempts of revolutionary leaders to mobilize previously docile masses via propaganda and manipulation, but also through the self-perpetuating nature of political participation. Political participation, and at its heart exposure to political information (tainted and biased as that information may be), enhances the ability to conceptualize and to develop more abstract understandings of the political system.[13] What results is not necessarily a "superior capacity for political discernment," as claimed by authors who are themselves products of post-revolutionary polities,[14] but rather a greater willingness to partake in political activities. The society as a whole thus becomes more politicized, more willing and able to take a critical look at the political environment. In a paradoxical development, this politicized society becomes on the one hand politically sophisticated, with its political senses having grown sharper due to the revolutionary experience, while on the other hand it becomes more dogmatic, with the rhetoric of revolutionary certainty replacing reasoned political discourse. The level of argument rises, but the underlying ideological dogmas remain unchanged.

Divisions in the Post-Revolutionary Society

The relationship between mass political participation and the rhetorical demagoguery that permeates political life in post-revolutionary societies is a fundamental one. Mass mobilization, exposure to risks, a sense of self-righteousness, the semblance of participatory democracy, and the sheer weight of the revolution as a dramatic historical event all lead to the development of a collective identity and solidarity which revolve around the revolutionary experience. "Movement identities create boundaries between an 'us' and a 'them'. From the beginning, (there are) sharp distinctions between two types of critics: those who (are) part of the movement and those who (are) not."[15]

In the process, "movement participants construct a 'we' that becomes, in varying degrees with different individuals, part of their own definition of self."[16] At the core of this identity are the ideals around which the group originally mobilized. When confronted with risks, the group's identity becomes all the more pulverized, its ideals assuming an almost sacred character.[17] In post-revolutionary societies, the solidarity of mobilized groups is reinforced by having withstood the harsh tests of the revolution. Even for those groups who are still in pursuit of control over the political machinery, their ideals have achieved a measure of victory over those prevalent in the Old Order.

Under such circumstances, the identity of the group supplants and replaces the identity of the individual. "When a collective identity becomes a central part of one's personal identity, group solidarity and personal honor become indistinguishable."[18] The espousal and propagation of values and political doctrines become central to the self-perceptions of most citizens in post-revolutionary societies. They identify themselves and are in turn identified by others by virtue of their positions on the burning political questions of the time. The identity of most becomes that propagated by the emerging, patrimonial, post-revolutionary state. In name if not in spirit, the Russians became staunch Leninists, the Chinese devout Maoists, the Iranians "Followers of the Imam's Path," and the Cubans all "Fidelistas." For the doctrinal diehards who refuse to recognize the legitimacy of the new victors' ideals, political dogmas become an even more central part of their identity. They consider the revolution to have been rightly theirs but usurped by others along the way. The most potent weapon these aspiring revolutionaries have is their ideology, the physical battle having been ruthlessly won by the revolution's real victors. In the uncompromising, indeed stifling atmosphere of the post-revolutionary environment, ideological demagoguery is all but inevitable.

The Continuance of Revolutionary Mobilization

Increased politicization, collective identity, mass participation, and demagoguery are in turn perpetuated by the self-sustaining nature of revolutionary mobilization itself. To begin with, even after success, people who are mobilized toward revolutionary goals tend to have a romanticized image of their "mission" and of the actual process of mobilization itself. Specifically, they tend to idealize the quality of social relationships in their movement, "at times reflecting wishful thinking about the way things ought to be."[19] The propaganda and inclusionary policies of the new government are not ineffective. They are, however, greatly complemented by the psychological needs of the populace to maintain their newly-found sense of self worth. The public at large wants to maintain its "sense of non-private, extrafamilial worth: a sense that one must be recognized as having intrinsic value and worth, not just to family and friends but to others in the larger society."[20] Moreover, throughout the larger society and specifically among the revolution's participants, struggle, with mobilization as its most mundane representation, can potentially become an end in itself.[21] The sacrifices for the revolution are not easily forgotten, particularly among those whose comrades fell while fighting for the revolutionary cause. "The dead live," it is said of revolutionary martyrs, "and, recognized by the revolution, continue to work on its behalf."[22] Political participation is, in itself, perceived to be one of the fruits of the revolution. Efforts to halt it or to gain control over it, as post-revolutionary states often do, are bound to meet with determined opposition. Similar to the popular desires to hold onto newly-won cultural liberties, there is much resentment against relinquishing previously non-existent political freedoms.

There is, lastly, a marked rise in the nationalistic sentiments which permeate post-revolutionary societies. Considerable euphoria is generated with the success of the revolutionary movement, the public frenzied with a sense of power rarely experienced before. For everyone involved, the "motherland" becomes the main source of inspiration and the principal reason for embarking on political activity. The term "Motherland," or some glorified version of it, becomes part of the routine vernacular of the day.[23] For the newly emerging political elite, love of the motherland becomes a particularly important means of maintaining popular support. In cases where international wars occur, whipping up nationalist sentiments becomes a crucial part of the political project.[24] But the manipulation of popular nationalist feelings becomes central to the consolidation of power against domestic enemies also, with non-conformists and dissidents being branded as traitors working to undermine the integrity of the motherland. More importantly, nationalist sentiments are often called on to justify the economic sacrifices which post-revolutionary states ask of their citizens.[25] At the same time, groups for whom the revolution has been hijacked justify their continued, extralegal pursuit of power not on grounds of merely wanting power but on grounds of a superior knowledge of what is right for the country. Whether truly a pawn of propaganda by both sides or genuinely taken by the euphoria of the revolutionary experience, the public is, in the meanwhile, also caught up in the nationalistic frenzy. The Motherland also becomes the center around which its universe revolves, the reason for its sacrifices, the jargon on its tongue.

It is within this overall context which post-revolutionary societies operate, at least in the immediate aftermath of revolutions. But for how long? Do societies endlessly experience these phenomena once they have undergone a revolution? There are no definitive answers to these questions, for a revolution or a specific aspect of it cannot be said to have ended say five or ten years after its success. Some revolutions never die, or at least unleash dynamics whose effects touch generations of lives. Most do, none the less, peter out at some point or another, their lingering social, cultural, and psychological (if not political) effects eventually eroded by the force of time. The polarization of the masses, both culturally and politically, eventually subsides. As wars end, whether fought domestically or internationally, so does euphoric nationalism subside and turns into an ordinary sense of attachment to the country. Demands for continued participation in the political process become routinized under inclusionary systems, concern with the fine aesthetics of political practice giving way to the realities of everyday life. The level of political discourse and conceptualization remain high, at least compared to pre-revolutionary times, but still carefully eyed by the political establishment. Perhaps most importantly, the conflictual relationship between the state and society turns into a consensual one, even if based upon force rather than voluntary compliance. In other words, the political culture of the state begins to take hold, forming the dominant milieu within which state-society relations are formulated. It is to the examination of this facet if post-revolutionary polities which we next turn.

POLITICAL CULTURE

Political culture has in recent years been subject to much scholarly debate and theorizing.[26] At the most elementary level, political culture refers to the cultural values that govern political behavior. In their pioneering work on the subject, Gabriel Almond and Sidney Verba defined political culture as the "particular distribution of patterns of orientation toward political objects among members of the nation."[27] They saw political culture as the connecting link between micro- and macro-politics, with popular political perceptions and orientations having direct bearing on a country's political institutions and prevailing patterns of political behavior.[28] Political culture affects "the conduct of individuals in their political roles, the content of their political demands, and their responses to laws."[29] In short, political culture is made up of the sum total of popular perceptions of the body politic. Needless to say, in revolutionary circumstances significant changes occur in the political culture. Indeed, a mutually reinforcing relationship develops between the post-revolutionary governing bodies on the one hand and the new, emerging political culture on the other. Political initiatives by the new elites foster new and radically different ways in which they are perceived by the public, while cultural traits with roots in both the ethos of revolution and the remnant of the pre-revolutionary era in turn nurture and strengthen evolving political forms.

Revolutions, it was earlier mentioned, are caused and in turn bring about a collapse of social control.[30] This is reversed by the reestablishment of the repressive capacities of the state, which, coercively if need be, devises, implements, and reinforces new norms for social, cultural and political conduct. In a sense, the post-revolutionary regime becomes domestically powerful enough to be able to superimpose its tailor-made political culture on the general population. This new political culture is not, of course, completely alien to the populace and its many nuances are, in fact, much more in tune with the sensibilities of the people than was ever the case with the political culture of the *ancien régime*. This is a political culture born out of a mass-based revolution, embodying the ethos of popular struggle. It is, in any case, one which by necessity harnesses politically inclusionary principles, ceaselessly striving to minimise any gaps that may appear between the masses and the political establishment. The distinction between the rhetorical "government of the masses" as a tool for political gimmickry and an actual reality indeed becomes increasingly blurred. Popular identification with the regime in fact becomes the most marked characteristic of the system.[31] The apparent marriage of society and the body politic at times becomes so pervasive that those subject to it cannot help but to idealize their predicament, perceiving themselves as participants in a highly democratic political culture. The following passage, written by two Cuban scholars, is representative of this type of idealization:

> The very evolution of citizen's political culture under the strong impact of the revolution has essentially modified the conditions for the exercise of participatory democracy and popular power in Cuba. The Cuban citizenry, independent of its ideological diversity, shares a complex political culture born out of the country's singular historical experience and developed and refined over three decades and has achieved a superior capacity for political discernment. These values, reinforced or constructed by the revolutionary process, are the fundamental substrate of potential change.[32]

But these are rather superficial observations regarding post-revolutionary political cultures. Beyond the perceptions of participatory democracy, what are the real characteristics which underlie the new ways in which society relates to the political establishment? How fundamental are the real changes which characterize the new, revolutionary political culture? Upon a closer inspection, it becomes evident that not all post-revolutionary political cultures radically differ from the ones they replace. The distinction most often lies in the symbolic representations of the two rather than in their contents.

Post-Revolutionary Political Change

Let us begin with a general overview of the nature and characteristics of post-revolutionary political cultures. As the preceding discussions have shown, such political cultures generally embody features that are conducive to mass political participation and collective behavior (aimed at inculcating a communal, collective identity), a highly charged political atmosphere, sensitivity on the part of the state toward popular political orientations, and deliberate efforts by the government designed to instill a set of politically-defined norms and values among its subjects. In his discussion of the political culture of post-revolutionary China, Lucian Pye has presented an analysis which, despite its contextual specificity, could apply to all post-revolutionary political cultures. Chinese political culture, he argues, is marked by

> sensitivity of authority to matters of 'face', the need for authority to omnipotence, the legitimacy of bewailing grievances, the urge to monopolize virtue and to claim the high ground of morality, the drive to try to shame others, an obsession with revenge, the inability to compromise publicly, and so on. All of which come down to a basic problem in Chinese political culture, the management of aggression. Any conflict arouses hate; i t becomes almost impossible to disagree politically without becoming disagreeable.[33]

These are traits that are not unique to the Chinese example. They are, to one extent or another, found almost universally in all post-revolutionary political cultures.

Two characteristics particularly stand out. The first is the all-engrossing nature of the political domain. Every facet of life, from the most mundane to the most personal, somehow becomes political. This is brought on by a confluence of government initiatives as well as general popular perceptions. On the one hand, post-revolutionary states are determined to give currency to their new values and symbols. Their zealous drive for symbolic and valuative legitimacy often touches the most personal aspects of the lives of their citizens. From marriage ceremonies to funeral processions, from naming new-born babies to choosing places of residence, everything becomes tied into the symbolic legitimacy of the new, revolutionary order.[34] In post-revolutionary Iran, for example, official condolence messages for war casualties which appeared in newspapers often congratulated the family of the deceased for having contributed a "martyr" to the revolutionary cause.[35]

This politicization of everyday life is in turn reinforced by a popular desire to seek for absolute truths in political terms. This is a population that has just been through a revolution, having a simplified perception of the historic, political dynamics that are at work. It sees few in-betweens, its universe revolving around resolute political dogmas that were hardened in the process of revolutionary mobilization and the ensuing, invariably bloody struggle. Both immediately prior to and after the revolution, the distinction between non-political and politically relevant events becomes increasingly blurred. Even natural disasters and other strictly non-political phenomena are somehow linked to the performance and the overall nature of the body politic.[36]

With revolutionary angers focused on political objects, political solutions are also sought for post-revolutionary answers. In popular minds, the connection between the overtly political and the tangentially so becomes much more accented, while even the completely non-political becomes somehow political. Matters both economic as well as aesthetic are popularly perceived to be politically related even if their connection is faint at best. Not only are such matters as crop harvests, the quality of bread and other basic food items, and the availability of sought-after consumer goods seen as directly related to the political domain, but so are such rather personal concerns as the timing and nature of marriages, family gatherings and relations among kinfolks, and orientations toward otherwise politically insignificant religious and cultural principles. Politics, in short, becomes an all-encompassing facet of daily life.

A second feature of post-revolutionary political cultures is their decidedly anti-democratic tilt. They are not, as clearly evident, political cultures that are conducive to democratic ideals or practices. Despite the rhetoric of the revolution, such political cultures are, in fact, highly rigid and inflexible with extreme dictatorial, indeed totalitarian, characteristics. The underlying reasons for the appearance of anti-democratic political cultures after revolutions are numerous and varied. To begin with, post-revolutionary political cultures often retain many of the underlying characteristics that they had prior to the revolution. In spite of zealous and often brutal attempts by post-revolutionary governments to inculcate new symbols and values, many of the dominant features of the pre-revolutionary political culture remain intact and carry over to the post-revolutionary era, at least in the immediate aftermath of the revolution. The political and cultural features that are most resistant to change are those with deep historical resonance, most notably, for example, those that breed cults of personality, authoritarianism, and a popular desire to mix religion and politics. In many cultural settings, these traits are too deeply rooted in daily life and the popular psyche to be easily altered through revolutionary shock therapy. Often, incoming revolutionary leaders capitalize on these very cultural traits, albeit under revolutionary auspices, in order to enhance their own stature and legitimacy. From Robespierre to Lenin, Stalin, Mao, Castro, and Khomeini, they all heavily relied on existing, pre-revolutionary cultural dynamics in consolidating their powers in the post-revolutionary era.[37]

Another reason for the anti-democratic tendencies found in post-revolutionary political cultures is the sense of certainty and moral righteousness which permeates them. Revolutionary leaders are, by nature, certain of what they want, often believing their cause to be sacred. They talk, act, and conduct themselves as if their mission is messianic and their message celestial. Many go so far as to deify themselves, trying, as Mao did, to become immortal by fusing their ego with the collective abstraction.[38] Revolutions involve mass mobilization, and mass mobilization involves belief, certainty, and conviction. The characteristics of the mobilized revolutionary activist are remarkably similar to those of the "authoritarian personality." Authoritarian personalities are "potentially fascist: conventional, submissive, unimaginative, superstitious, mystical, rigid and stereotyped in thinking, preoccupied with power and toughness, cynical and destructive, misanthropic, and projective. . . . "[39] The lower classes and the displaced rural population, who often form the bulk of the mobilized masses, tend to be most authoritarian.[40] On the whole, these authoritarian characters are

> less educated and less intelligent than the average, but more rigid and concrete in their thinking even (if) more intelligent than the average. They (are) more intolerant of ambiguity and (are) superstitious, suggestible, and autistic, while democratic personalities (show) greater creativity, imagination, and ability for empathy.[41]

With these characteristics come a sense of moral righteousness, a stern belief in a unique understanding of truth. Considering the drama and intensity of revolutions, there often develops a sense that idealistic, revolutionary ends justify the means. In the process, most of the democratic ideals for which revolutions invariably stand are trampled upon. A cultural milieu is formed in which ideological rigidity, dogmatism, cults of personality, messianic tendencies, and the justification of ends by means are dominant. Democracy is preached by the revolutionary government but practiced by neither itself nor its subjects. Inclusionary policies perpetuate a semblance of democratic practices, but as an actual, culturally accepted and ingrained force, democracy remains at best an elusive ideal.

Revolution and Popular Perception

The persistence of anti-democratic trends in post-revolutionary political cultures (due to pre-revolutionary characteristics) does not automatically mean that political cultures do not undergo far-reaching, revolutionary transformations. Indeed, *revolutionary* political cultures are often just that, revolutionary. They are considerably different from the static and inert cultures that they replace. Not only are their symbolic representations different, but so are their basic tenets in terms of popular perceptions of the body politic. In the inclusionary political systems that develop after successful revolutions, people *envision* themselves as participants in a democratic process, although the political arena may indeed be highly rigid and stifling. The political culture, those popular perceptions that people have of the political establishment, is dramatically changed. People perceive the political system much more favorably, and in fact see the act of engaging in politics in a completely different light. No longer is "politicking" frowned on as it was prior to the revolution, no longer are politicians seen as vain and corrupt. Politics becomes a passionate field of activity devoted to the betterment of mankind; its artisans, the politicians, are revolutionary heroes committed to bringing about a better life. People identify with these rebels-*cum*-leaders much more readily. They feel, on the whole, closer to the political establishment, indeed perceiving themselves as an integral part of the political process. Post-revolutionary leaders also often have a greater degree of what one scholar calls "solidary relations with the broader strata."[42] Even if they find it necessary to resort to violence and coercion to legitimize their newly-won powers (and that they frequently do), they still retain a much closer relationship to the masses than pre-revolutionary leaders ever did. The post-revolutionary political culture is, in the final analysis, different from the one it replaces in many but not all facets, some of its underlying themes remaining intact while others are radically changed.

DISSENT AND OPPOSITION

Given the nature of post-revolutionary systems, societies, and political cultures, is the formulation and development--if not necessarily the expression--of dissent and opposition possible? The break-up of the successful revolutionary coalition and the ensuing violence during the reign of terror is a "natural corollary" of the revolutionary process.[43] But are opposition movements emerging outside of the revolutionary coalition also possible? Post-revolutionary political systems are inclusionary at best and totalitarian at worst, supported by political cultures with anti-democratic tendencies. With the regime embarking on an intense propaganda campaign in order to attain legitimacy, supported by its lack of inhibitions in resorting to coercive means to enhance its strength, political opposition is stifled and not given much breathing room. Opposition is also stifled culturally, its message finding little purchase in a cultural environment permeated by rigid, inflexible, and authoritarian tendencies. Is there, however, still a possibility that moves to oppose the revolutionary establishment be made by the various social strata?

Post-Revolution Opposition

Opposition to revolutionary establishments is, indeed, a distinct possibility. In fact, despite (and often because of) the rigid conformism that characterizes post-revolutionary polities, flares of opposition to the political establishment commonly appear, at times with great intensity. Even if the new regime can effectively suppress the *expression* of oppositional sentiments, there are still dynamics at work which allow such sentiments to be formulated amongst certain groups. Yet such underlying sentiments often boil into the surface and, even if for only a brief interlude, result in intense and violent conflicts. The source of such oppositional sentiments can be traced to three specific centers. They include, broadly, the extent of activism by remnant elites of the Old Order, the counter-revolutionaries; the degree of isolation of the new elites from the popular classes; and the intensity and direction of the politicization of previously docile masses. Either individually or in combination with one another, these developments combine to accentuate the volatility of the political atmosphere following a revolution. There is, nevertheless, a clear difference between the nature and extent of anti-government sentiments before the revolution as opposed to afterward. Prior to the success of revolutionary movements, anti-governmental sentiments are relatively widespread and, even if at times muted by the coercive arms of the state, are held deeply enough to facilitate mobilization and revolutionary agitation. The type of anti-establishment sentiment that is being discussed here, however, has at best a highly narrow base, its propagators and adherents forming a distinct minority among a vast majority of vocal and active pro-government supporters.

The politicization of previously non-political groups has been previously alluded to but is worth recounting here. Following revolutions, the political atmosphere is intensely charged and polarized. This polarization is further accentuated by the incessant propaganda of not only the new political elite but also those of revolutionary hopefuls who still find themselves excluded from the new institutional arrangements. Inclusionary practices are adopted not only by the government but also by the various politicized, non-governmental groups. Groups left out of the political formula carry forward their campaign to muster public support more zealously than ever before, in the process finding the charged political environment conducive to their ends. New political parties emerge, each claiming to spearhead a radical cause. Many such parties concentrate on peripheral issues, taking advantage of the tenuous position of post-revolutionary states in order to press for specific, narrowly-based ethnic and regional demands. Resenting the efforts of post-revolutionary states to re-impose central authority on the country, such parties, even if not necessarily regionally based, spearhead the cause of regional issues--autonomy, the right to teach the local dialect in schools, the right to control the local police force, refusal to be conscripted into the national army, and so on. These regional rebellions take place at a critical time in the life of the post-revolutionary state, when their powers are most tenuous: immediately after they have been established but before having had sufficient time to consolidate themselves. For a time, civil wars and the disintegration of the nation seem imminent. Civil wars were indeed part of the immediate aftermaths of the French, Russian, Chinese, and Iranian revolutions. In all cases, however, these regionally-based conflicts were settled in favor of revolutionary elites once they had fully consolidated their powers.[44]

The re-establishment of the coercive capacities of the state and its ability to effectively exert authority over its citizens, which in post-revolutionary circumstances occur with considerable brutality, is in turn directly related to the degree which the new political elites are isolated from the general population. This *initial* isolation--inclusionary polities soon lessening the gap between the political elite and the populace-- is more probable in political systems resulting from planned revolutions than spontaneous ones, in which the revolutionary leaders are from the start perceived to be inseparable from the masses. The gap between the elite and the masses, at a time when the latter is trying to impose a new set of institutions and values on society, is a potential cause for friction. "The more autonomous such elites are," according to one observer,

> lacking close solidary ties with other elites or groups, and the more antagonistic they are to the major social strata, the more the new institutional complexes will be restructured and the smaller the extent of autonomous access of other groups to positions of control. The more autonomous such elites are, enjoying either adaptive or solidary relations with broader groups, the more they will be able to develop coalitions with other relatively autonomous elites, as was the case in Europe and to some extent Turkey.[45]

In such circumstances, where the new elites have little valuative legitimacy among the politically active population, the possibility of opposition activity is great.

Apart from the possibility of opposition by elites seeking to share in the political fruits of the revolution, opposition is likely from those remaining elements that were in one way or another tied to the Old Order. When politically active, they are, by nature, counter-revolutionary, their prime purpose being the containment and eventual reversal of the revolution. Counter-revolutionary opposition to the post-revolutionary state is an inevitable phase of the revolutionary process. This is, however, an opposition that is neither forceful nor determined, its cause being one with little purchase and popularity. Its task is to reverse the course of history, but its effort is faint and uninspired. As the military ventures of the White Russians showed, the efforts of such counter-revolutionaries are more cause for celebration among the revolution's foreign enemies rather than a real domestic threat.[46] These are, after all, members of the former elite, accustomed to a pampered life, not political activism and revolutionary agitation. Their main strength is neither their resolve nor their popularity but rather their comparatively vast financial resources. Even with their economic power, they are hardly in a position to finance acts of violence against the revolutionary regime. Most are, in fact, no longer a real force inside their own country, having often been compelled to leave for exile or a safe haven. The most they can do is to use their money to fuel their propaganda campaign against the New Order, a campaign with more listeners and adherents outside of the country rather than inside.

As the foregoing analysis demonstrates, dissent and opposition within post-revolutionary regimes is politically possible, and in fact prevalent, but socially and culturally vacuous. Despite its vibrance and newly-found zest, the post-revolutionary political culture is too much a captive of the new power elite to allow for unsolicited expressions of political opinion. The level of conceptualization may have changed. The caliber of political discourse may have progressed. Counter-revolutionaries sing their usual songs; and long suppressed regional demands find temporary breathing room. But the underlying characteristics of the political establishment, those which nurture anti-democratic tendencies and disallow the expression of conflicting views, remain the same. Dissidents are crushed with an intensity rarely seen in the pre-revolutionary era. Counter-revolutionaries and would-be separatists are punished the hardest, all victims of a burgeoning police state.[47] The post-revolutionary state eventually triumphs, subduing all social groups which seek its overthrow. In the process, it shapes the social and cultural forces which govern the lives of its citizens.

CONCLUSION

Revolutions alter not just political institutions and practices but the very inner reaches of civil society as well. They change the ground rules on which social interactions are based, the perceptions that society has of the state and the manner in which the two interact, and the very direction in which social and cultural norms point. Revolutions consume the polity in totality, not just politically or socially but also culturally and psychologically. Few of the citizens are left untouched by the enormity of the revolution, their lives having changed forever by its deeply penetrating affects. They not only see political objects differently but have a different perception of themselves and of their place within the political drama. People even think differently, having achieved a measure of intellectual sophistication due to the sheer weight of the revolutionary experience.

Admittedly, the most conspicuous of revolutionary changes occur in the symbolic representations of the political establishment. They are, however, by no means the only change that engulf the post-revolutionary polity. The dominant frames of political and cultural reference become unsettled, necessitating considerable normative and practical adjustments on the part of the general population. People need to learn and be familiarized with new political forms and symbols, accept their legitimacy, and make them part of their routine, daily contact with the body politic. But this is at best a highly traumatic experience, involving fundamental shifts in the way people perceive and relate to the political universe around them. Many, in fact, refuse to voluntarily adopt the valuative dictums that are being handed out to them, despite an overwhelming campaign by the regime to give currency to its new political and cultural medians. "Dissynchronization of values" occurs, leading ultimately to political instability and violence.[48]

Yet another revolution is out of the question. Merely sharp and rigid disagreements develop between the values propagated by the emerging power elite on the one hand and those of a vocal though ultimately doomed minority of political activists on the other. This minority of political non-conformists is eventually silenced, passively submitting to the authority of the state if not becoming part of its vast pool of vocal supporters.

The forced imposition of new political values and institutions result in two specific developments. First and foremost, it results in a violent and brutal turnover of the elite, not just physically in political and economic terms, but also in terms of the constant ridiculing of their values and beliefs and their replacement with alternative, revolutionary ones. In so far as the former elite's values are concerned, they are portrayed by the new leaders as corrupt, historically anachronistic, exploitative, and wanting in morality. It is, in fact, precisely these values which the revolutionary leaders' most interested in eradicating. They correctly view the abolition of such values and their replacement with alternative, revolutionary ones as pivotal to their success.

These new values and normative principles are radically different from the ones they replace. Regardless of what the pre-revolutionary social and cultural values might have had at their heart, the new values governing the post-revolutionary society are decidedly more puritanical, with much greater pretence to upholding the betterment of the entire society. They are marked by an unprecedented sense of morality, the upholding of high ethics, and a sense of communal spirit and suppression of individualism. But most revolutionary elites do not stop here. For many, the actual physical elimination of those related to the former rulers becomes a main revolutionary project. Guillotines, labor camps, hangings, and firing squads become the order of the day. To elaborate on the misfortunes that befall members of the old elite would be redundant; suffice it to say here that most are eliminated in both name and in spirit.

The Old Elite Flees

To avoid persecution, those members of the former elite who have the ability of doing so emmigrate. Many flee from real danger; many others flee because of the possibility of danger. Still others leave because they find the new political and cultural environments unbearable. These emmigrants invariably make their way into countries where they find the political establishment sympathetic to their plight. Cultural proximity, if not outright similarity, does not hurt. What results is a growing community of *emigres* largely made up of wealthy former elites. They are, by nature, invariably opposed the revolutionary system in place back in their mother country. Similar to despotic systems and counter-revolutionaries, *emigre* communities soon become a natural by-product of revolutions. Just as the French and Russian revolutions led to the appearance of *emigre* communities in Austria-Hungary and Germany respectively, so did the Cuban and Iranian revolutions lead to the development of *emigre* communities in the U.S. Similarly, an *emigre* Algerian community formed in France soon after Algeria's revolutionary war of independence from that country.[49] Regardless of their specific predicaments, most *emigres* are soon resigned to the fact that their place in history has forever been lost and adopt their place of residence as their own. A few, however, continue to entertain thoughts of defeating the revolution and become members in a vocal but ineffective counter-revolutionary movement.

Vociferous propaganda by counter-revolutionaries is only one of the less significant ramifications of the old elite's flight abroad. Their emmigration can potentially have much more immediate negative ramifications for the fledgling political system they leave behind. They do, after all, tend to form the most wealthy segment of the population, often controlling key industries and sources of investment. Their flight may expedite the institutionalization of new political elites as it severs the last vestiges of the Old Order, but it also results in a direct and very conspicuous flight of capital. The stakes are not just opulent lifestyles, consumerist attitudes, and international market connections. The results are much more far reaching and consequential for the domestic economy. Whether through voluntary departure from the country or forced property confiscation, the country's economic magnates are dispossessed, no longer capable of supporting the peripheral, informal economic networks that often revolve around them. Handymen, hangers-on, maids, and servants--and in Republican China personal armies--all suffer economically as a result of the disintegration of the old elites. Most are sooner or later reintegrated into the labor force, often serving as the revolution's foot-soldiers in one of the government's inclusionary campaigns. But their temporary redundancy and dislocation is both large-scale and trying, bringing about considerable economic hardships on those who can least withstand it.

At the same time, the dispersion of the old economic elite and the ensuing flight of capital result in a dampening of entrepreneurial spirits, compounded by the government's anti-individualistic rhetoric. The magnates who leave (or are compelled to leave) are often big industrialists, stewards of the ethics of capitalist competition and enterprise. Their departure from the scene of economic activity, coupled with the government's lofty promises of a better future and its campaign to inculcate communal values, impede the chances for a regeneration of the economy. All of these difficulties are further compounded by a brain-drain, with the elite's most educated and skilled members leaving for safe havens. Doctors and engineers join the wave of wealthy merchants, industrialists, and high-ranking military and civilian officials streaming out of the country.[50] The effects of such wholesale immigrations for the revolutionary country's economy and social welfare are little short of devastating.

The Psychological Ramifications of Revolution

The second ramification of the forced imposition of revolutionary norms and values is far less tangible, and thus harder to discern. It involves a "psychic split," a dichotomy of the citizen's self-identity between an ardent supporter of "the cause" on the one hand and an ordinary individual on the other. Similar to those living under totalitarian systems, the individual develops what one observer calls a "true" and a "false" self.

> An appropriately modulated false self protects the true self from environmental threats; the false self permits the true self to act only during those moments when success, if not assured, is probable; it allows the true self to live secretly, silently. In this sense, the false sense encompasses an appropriate and necessary 'polite and mannered social attitude.' After all, the 'spontaneous gestures' may not always be functional. More colloquially, at times the true self needs a mask behind which to hide. Therefore, individuals quite naturally have a public and a private self.[51]

Political prudence often dictates behavior which may not necessarily be heart-felt, or a behavior which, even if voluntary, is intensified by the force of circumstances. In post-revolutionary circumstances, the split between the public and the private self may not be as accentuated as is the case in totalitarian systems, of the kind that existed in Eastern Europe before 1989 for example, but it does, none the less, exist. Post-revolutionary societies are characterized by a new sense of identity wrapped in nationalism, revolutionary symbols, and the worship of revolutionary heroes both dead and alive. The new, post-revolutionary political culture does support these premises, giving them a genuine measure of popularity among the population. However, as the revolution ages and its zeal subsides, as its message begins to tire even the most devout, whole-hearted adherence to its ideals becomes more and more of a facade. To survive, those who engage in overt political activity have no alternative but to adopt a split self, whether consciously or subconsciously.[52]

The development of a "psychic split" serves to epitomize the very depth to which revolutions affect and change the polities in which they occur. Revolutions may be initially sparked by distinctively political phenomena, but their affects and ramifications are in no way limited to the political domain. They touch societies both as a whole and at a personal level, altering the individual lives of citizens. Whether making them political activists for the first time or enhancing their ability to think and conceptualize politically, be it subjecting them to a split personality or forcing their emmigration, in one way or another, revolution changes the daily activities in which people engage. Because of it, many feel better about themselves, having achieved the impossible and in the process acquired a new sense of identity and self-worth. Others feel betrayed, angered at their former comrades for stealing the harvests they feel rightly belongs to them.   Still others seek to reverse the tide of the revolution, scheming ways to restore past glory and power. A few stand on the sidelines, marvelling at the perceived savagery of the drama being played around them. And yet, like it or not, they too are players in this drama, unwittingly pushing forward the historical resonance of the revolution.

Notes

1. Throughout this chapter, "polity" is taken to mean a combination of the body politic and civil society, the totality of the political system and society together.

2. S.N. Eisenstadt, *Revolution and the Transformation of Societies* (New York: Free Press, 1978), p. 217.

3. John Dunn, *Modern Revolutions: Introduction to the Analysis of a Political Phenomenon* 2nd ed. (Cambridge: Cambridge University Press, 1988), p. 239.

4. Eisenstadt, *Revolution and Transformation of Societies*, p. 218.

5. For an examination of the links between cultural change and political violence, see Chalmers Johnson, *Revolutionary Change*, 2nd ed. (London: Longman, 1982), especially Chaps. 2, 3, and 4.

6. Crane Brinton, *The Anatomy of Revolution* (New York: Prentice-Hall, 1952), p. 200.

7. For a brief examination of Stalin's Cultural Revolution, see Sheila Fitzpatrick, *The Russian Revolution, 1917-1932* (Oxford: Oxford University Press, 1982), pp. 129-34; for the Chinese Cultural Revolution, see Immanuel Hsu. *The Rise of Modern China* 4th ed. (Oxford: Oxford University Press, 1990), pp. 658-60; for Iran, see Mehran Kamrava, *From Tribalism to Theocracy: The Political History of Modern Iran* (New York: Praeger, 1993), Chap. 4.

8. For a discussion of state-sponsored violence in post-revolutionary Iran see Kamrava, *From Tribalism to Theocracy*, Chap. 4.

9. For a discussion of women's roles and issues in post-revolutionary Iran see Farah Azari, "The Post-Revolutionary Women's Movement in Iran," Farah Azari, ed., *Women of Iran: The Conflict with Fundamentalist Islam* (London: Ithaca Press, 1983), pp. 190-225.

10. See Kate Millet, *Going to Iran* (New York: Coward, McCann & Geoghegan).

11. Irma Adelman and Jarius Hihn, "Crisis Politics in Developing Countries," *Economic Development and Cultural Change* vol. 33, no. 1 (October 1984), p. 20.

12. Jerrold Green, "Counter Mobilization as a Revolutionary Form," *Comparative Politics* vol. 16, no. 2 (January 1984), p. 157.

13. Jan Leighley, "Participation as a Stimulus for Political Conceptualization," *The Journal of Politics* vol. 53, no. 1 (February 1991), p. 207.

14. Dunn, *Modern Revolutions*, p. 53.

15. William Gamson, "Commitment and Agency in Social Movement," *Sociological Forum* vol 6, no. 1 (1991), p. 42.

16. Ibid, p. 45.

17. Ibid.

18. Ibid, p. 46.

19. Ibid, p. 47.

20. James Davies, "Maslow and Theory of Political Development: Getting to Fundamentals," *Political Psychology* vol. 12, no. 3 (1991), p.

400.

21. The concept of "ethics of struggle" is elaborated on, though in a different context, in Tom Denyer, "The Ethics of Struggle," *Political Theory* vol. 17, no. 4 (November 1989), pp. 535-49. Relevant to this discussion, however, is Denyer's assertion that "as a practical matter, an ethics of struggle can be produced and evaluated in the course of the struggle itself." p. 536.

22. B.E. Aguirre, "The Conventionalization of Collective Behavior in Cuba," *American Journal of Sociology* vol. 90, no. 3 (1984), p. 560.

23. The glorification of nationalism in Stalinist Soviet Union is insightfully discussed in Roy Medvedev, *Let History Judge: The Origins and Consequences of Stalinism* (New York: Alfred Knopf, 1971), p. 518-19. Stalin, Medvedev points out, justified the actions of even the most notorious historical Russian leaders, including Ivan the Terrible, not very different, he continues, from the glorification of Genghis Khan in Maoist China.

24. Wars, as discussed in chapter three, are common occurrences following revolutions, not only because revolutions tend to upset the immediate regional balance of power but also because post-revolutionary states have immense power to mobilize citizens for wars.

25. See above, chapter 3.

26. See Stephen Chilton, "Defining Political Culture," *Western Political Quarterly* vol 41, no 3 (September 1988), pp. 419-45.

27. Gabriel Almond and Sidney Verba, *The Civic Culture* (London: Sage, 1989), p. 13.

28. Ibid, p. 32.

29. Ibid, p. 25.

30. Dunn, *Modern Revolutions*, p. 239.

31. Samuel Huntington, *Political Order in Changing Societies* (New Haven, CT: Yale University Press, 1968), p. 310.

32. Rafael Hernandez and Harolda Dilla, "Political Culture and Popular Participation in Cuba," *Latin American Perspectives* vol. 18, no. 2 (Spring 1991), p. 53.

33. Lucian Pye, "Tienanmen and Chinese Political Culture," *Asian Survey* vol. 30, no. 4 (April 1990), pp. 331-2.

34. See above, Chap. 3.

35. Examples of such glorifications of martyrdom in revolutionary Iran (which is, incidentally, a relatively recent development within Islam) can be seen in the government-published booklet entitled *Eslam, Maktab-e Mubarez* (Islam, the Combatant Religion) (Tehran: n.p., 1358/1979).

36. Depending on the political mood dominating the population in terms of popular support for the regime (or lack thereof, as the case

may be), the government's capacity to deliver and its functional viability is put to test at such times of crisis. As a result, the same population that may see the relief activities of an incumbent, pre-revolutionary regime as lackluster and incompetent may perceive the identical efforts of a popular, post-revolutionary government as heroic, unprecedented, and genuinely dedicated.

37. This continuity is discussed in specific relation to Russian history and the Soviet system in Robert Daniels, "Russian Political Culture and the Post-Revolutionary Impasse," *The Russian Review* vol. 47, (1987), pp. 165-76.

38. Lowell Dittmer, "Mao and the Politics of Revolutionary Morality," *Asian Survey* vol. 27, no. 3 (March 1987), p. 335.

39. William Eckhardt, "Authoritarianism," *Political Psychology* vol. 12, no. 1, (1991), p. 108.

40. Ibid, p. 109.

41. Ibid.

42. Eisenstadt, *Revolution and the Transformation of Societies*, p. 243.

43. Ernest Gellner, *Plough, Sword, and Book: The Structure of Human History*.(Chicago: University of Chicago Press, 1988), p. 147.

44. It can be argued that the post-revolutionary Chinese did not achieve a complete victory in the ensuing civil war since they were unable to suppress the Nationalist control of Taiwan.

45. Eisenstadt, *Revolution and the Transformation of Societies*, p. 246.

46. For more on the White Russian armies, see Sheila Fitzpatrick, *The Russian Revolution, 1917-1932*, pp. 67-9.

47. Ted Gurr, "War, Revolution, and the Growth of the Coercive State," *Comparative Political Studies* vol. 21, no. 1 (April 1988), p. 53.

48. See Johnson, *Revolutionary Change*.

49. For a discussion of the French *emigres* see R. Ben Jones, *The French Revolution* (London: Hodder & Stoughton, 1967), pp. 75-8; for Iranian *emigres*, see Mehdi Bozorgmehr and Georges Sabagh, "High Status Immigrants: A Statistical Profile of Iranians in the United States," *Iranian Studies* vol. 21, nos. 3-4 (1988), pp. 5-35.

50. See for example, Bozorgmehr and Sabagh, "High Status Immigrants."

51. Eric Scheye, "Psychological Notes on Central Europe: 1989 and Beyond," *Political Psychology* vol. 12, no. 2 (1991), p. 334.

52. Ibid, p. 337.

5

Conclusion

Revolutions are dramatic episodes in the political history of the nations in which they occur. They alter fundamental aspects of not only prevailing political, social, cultural, and economic arrangements but the very personal lives of the citizens involved as well. As the preceding chapters demonstrated, revolutions are caused primarily by a coalescence of political, social, cultural, and diplomatic factors. Politically, revolutions will not succeed unless the state in which they take place is confronted with fundamental systemic problems which make its collapse imminent. The mobilization of broad strata of society toward specifically revolutionary goals is equally important, brought about by both situational links between revolutionary groups and the general masses on the one hand and deep-seated grievances which make society susceptible to revolutionary mobilization on the other. Once they do succeed, revolutions bring about political institutions that are inherently stronger and more reliant on coercion than the ones they replace. New leaders emerge following what is often an extremely brutal and violent struggle among former comrades, forging new institutional and cultural norms as part of a campaign to establish a New Order. They often confront determined dissent and opposition from groups whose hopes and aspirations, as well as level of political thinking, had reached a high pitch during the revolutionary process. Seldom, however, are post-revolutionary systems seriously challenged, at least domestically, most outlasting the nostalgic dreams of counter-revolutionaries.

This concluding chapter aims to bring some of the analytical questions regarding revolutions into sharper focus. Broadly, such questions concern the genesis, nature, and outcome of what could for the sake of analytical convenience be called "the revolutionary project." It is, for example, worth raising the question once again of whether revolutions begin voluntarily or non-voluntarily? Do revolutions have clearly defined goals? And if they do, how much correspondence is there between revolutionary outcomes and objectives and aspirations? Once they succeed, do revolutions result in political development? Before answering these questions, a brief recapping of the "revolutionary project" is in order.

THE REVOLUTIONARY PROJECT

Revolutions, as the preceding chapters demonstrate, come about as a result of dynamics that are engendered both in the prevailing political structures and the social and cultural make-up of population. That they require a weakened political machinery (weak in relation to society, that is) is a given. The causes of that weakness may be indigenous and endemic to the political system or the result of international dynamics (wars, for example), but at any rate they need to occur concurrent with social and cultural developments which make revolutionary mass mobilization feasible and its success probable. Revolutions necessitate the existence and formulation of grievances at the social level, be they based on frustrated political or economic aspirations or a confusion over the appropriate set of values to adopt. They cannot, however, be reduced to the efforts of people who some psychologists call "chronic protestors."[1] Invariably, they are brought about and in turn accentuate popular feelings of nationalism, best represented by the innate message of slogans which gain widespread (though for the most part admittedly temporary) currency during times of revolutionary upheaval. Concurrent with a rise in love for "the Motherland" is a rise in the popularity of ideologies that in ordinary times are considered "revolutionary"--Marxism-Leninism is a prime example--or of ideologies which assume an increasingly

revolutionary flavor though they may be static in other times--
Islam, for example. Sooner or later, at any rate, an ideology grows
to become the dominant theme of the revolution, embodying the
main language within which demands for the attainment of a
New Society are formulated.

The success of the revolutionary movement ushers in a new
era, one in which even the most mundane facets of life are
revolutionized. The state, by nature weak prior to the start of
the revolutionary movement, now grows in its strength, its
intrusive powers, and its reliance on and willingness to use
coercion. Much of this surge in power comes from the incorporation
of previously-excluded masses into the political process, as well
as the prevalence of new social and political norms and ideals.
Society is itself revolutionized, its norms and values, orientations
and ways of conduct having radically changed from what they
were before the revolution. Its ability to think and conceptualize
about politics becomes more sophisticated, and its eagerness to
partake in political activity more enthusiastic. Existing social
and political cleavages that divide society grow in the
meanwhile, muted by the ever-increasing coercive powers of the
state. Mass political incorporation enhances the seemingly
popular mandate of the revolutionary state, though it also
aggravates those groups for whom the revolution has been
betrayed and its continued struggle deemed essential. Grudgingly,
however, all corners of society inevitably succumb to the will of
the revolutionary state.

Whether revolutions start voluntarily or are the result of
largely uncontrollable social and political dynamics depends on
the exact nature of the revolution in question. Some begin as
carefully-planned programs for the overthrow of existing
political arrangements and the subsequent establishment of new
ones. In these instances, which are often the result of guerrilla
warfare, the original objectives and the outcome of the revolution
correspond most closely, with the revolutionaries implementing
upon their success previously laid-out blueprints for social and
political conduct.

Other revolutions, however, involve greater spontaneity,
with oppositional activists being propelled into positions of
revolutionary leadership as a result of a series of developments
which they originally did not have much to do with. In such

cases, revolutionary aspirations and demands are formulated as
an embryonic oppositional movement snowballs into a full-blown
revolution, growing in momentum as situational opportunities
facilitate mobilization and expedite the collapse of a dying
state. At least in their initial stages, these revolutions do not
have clear objectives--indeed they do not have clear leaders--
and revolutionary goals and aspirations are at best summed up
and expressed in vague, catch-all slogans. The general
population, meanwhile, or at least significant segments of it,
participates in revolutions voluntarily, though their negative
attitudes toward the Old Order are already largely shaped by
the existence of what they perceive to be exploitative economic
and political arrangements.

Another analytical question that needs to be addressed is
the relationship between revolutions and political development.
Revolutions, it is understood, engulf political establishments
that are not characterized by high degrees of development. Most
pre-revolutionary regimes are exclusionary, neopatrimonial,
narrowly based, and often excessively reliant on coercion for their
survival. Their political institutions are unevolved at best. Given
these characteristics, do revolutions result in the establishment
of a "more developed" political system? Barring value
judgements about the superiority of pre- and post-revolutionary
political systems, can the latter indeed be considered as
politically more evolved or developed as compared to the
former?

"Political Development" and Political Evolution

The concept of "political development" provides an
analytically useful tool for measuring the evolution of a political
system as it encounters a revolution. In broad terms, political
development entails a concurrent process whereby the powers of
the state grow and its institutions become increasingly
differentiated. "Political development," maintains one observer,
"has advanced if the amount of power available to a society
grows with no worsening of the distribution of power...."[2] More
specifically, it involves the capacity to allow for regularized
and systemic participation by broad strata of society. Some have
in fact defined political development in terms of an enhanced

capacity to allow for political participation. They see it as

> the process of admitting all groups and all interests, including newly recognized interests and new generations, into full political participation without disrupting the efficient working of the political system and without limiting the ability of the system to choose and pursue policy goals.[3]

Thus a system can be considered as politically developed if it has attained a

> qualitatively new and enhanced political capacity as manifested in the successful institutionalization of (1) new patterns of integration and penetration regulating and containing the tensions and conflicts produced by increased differentiation, and (2) new patterns of participation and resource distribution adequately responsive to the demands generated by the imperatives of equality.[4]

In this context, "equality" can be measured in terms of its three components of national citizenship, achievement norms, and a universalist legal order.[5]

As more recent studies have shown, however, political development connotes changes more fundamental than merely systemic and structural alterations. It involves transformations in the "cognitive structures underlying culture," or, more simply, in popular perceptions and expectations of the political system.[6] The main locus of political development is, therefore, political culture (not to be confused with individual culture or social systems).[7] Consequently, the process involves more than unilinear changes in political structures and institutions; multilinear changes in cultural contents also take place, bringing about new ways of relating to both specific institutions and the overall community.[8] In addition to the evolution of political institutions-- enhanced power capacities, structural differentiations, and a comparatively greater capacity for absorbing popular participation--the population experiences a general "cognitive growth," because of which previously-felt intellectual ambiguities are resolved.[9] There is also a normative aspect involved, with a more developed political system being one that is generally "better" than one that is not developed.[10]

Revolutions usher in political systems that appear to have undergone the process of "development." Post-revolutionary states may or may not be normatively "better" than the ones they replace. They are, however, no doubt structurally stronger and institutionally more differentiated than their preceding, pre-revolutionary systems. In such instances, power is far more centralized than ever before, and coercion becomes one of the main supporting pillars of the incoming elite. Moreover, post-revolutionary regimes foster and are in turn legitimized by entirely new forms of political culture and means of political and communal identification. New symbols replace the old; values and political orientations change. Insofar as popular participation is concerned, that is indeed where revolutions excel the most, often in fact turning the popular fervor of revolutionary followers into fanatical crusades against real or imagined enemies. Thus at least insofar as the aforementioned definitions are concerned, revolutions do bring about political development. But an important analytical distinction needs to be made here. For revolutions are at best spasmatic aberrations in the lives of political systems. They are infrequent and occur only within highly specific political and historic contexts. In a classic sense, they are both extremely condensed and magnified episodes of political development and in turn further its cause. Yet their effects are not always conducive to a regularized and systemic manner in which successively higher stages of political development are achieved.

Insofar as the relationship between political development and revolution is concerned, two specific developments are possible. First, a revolution could, theoretically at least, result in the establishment of a system that is not only politically more developed but one which also continues to engage in an ongoing process of political development on an evolutionary basis. The French and the American revolutions, for example, continued to evolve until their post-revolutionary regimes eventually matured into highly developed, democratic systems. Due to the very manner in which these systems have evolved, they engender forces that are capable of continued changes and evolutionary transformations. Moreover, there is a degree of unanimity among the citizens involved that the emerging post-revolutionary state is normatively "better" than the one it replaced, although an average Frenchman living during the Reign of Terror might take issue with that. At least in so far as the revolutionaries are concerned, most do set out to establish a New Order that is "better." But even if concrete examples are hard to come by--and the French revolution is *not* a terribly good one--it is theoretically possible to envision the establishment of a post-revolutionary state that is stronger, structurally more developed, and normatively better than its preceding one. Thus in such instances, the relationship between political development and revolution becomes a direct, mutually reinforcing one.

Few actual historical examples correspond to the theoretical aspirations of revolutionaries, however. In fact, as was demonstrated in chapter three, post-revolutionary systems are almost invariably dictatorial, coercive, and inflexible. Very few revolutions bring about political systems that are inherently changeable. Even in the French example cited above, one needs to take a pretty long, historical view of the revolution in order to be able to establish a linkage between that event and the eventual establishment of democracy. Revolutions do bring about more coercive states and radically different political cultures. The successor states are not always structurally more differentiated or higher up on a real or imaginary evolutionary scale. Moreover, their essentially different characteristics from those of the pre-revolutionary times do not necessarily translate into systems that are somehow "better" or more evolved. This point is often diluted by the assumption of modern-sounding titles and institutions by incoming revolutionary elites. Kings and sultans are brushed aside by presidents; general secretaries and party central committees replace presidents-for-life and other dictators. For certain elites the New Order may be far "better" than the old. But in so far as the general public is concerned, the New Order is often hardly more benign or benevolent than the one it replaced. Even a sense of popular democracy that is brought on by the new regime's inclusionary policies cannot hide the New Order's essentially stifling hold on society. At least in the immediate aftermath of revolution, it becomes all but an impossibility to assess the normative superiority of the New Order compared to the past. In this sense, the connection between revolution and political development is a narrow one.

Democratic Rhetoric, Dictatorial Results

It is here where the connection between revolutions and democracy becomes most tenuous. The rhetoric of revolution invariably calls for the establishment of democracy, even if only for the proletariat, but the outcome is often an inescapable dictatorship, whether permanent or temporary. By nature, revolutions lead to the establishment of political systems that are antithetical to democratic norms, practices, and institutions. No revolution, it is safe to argue, has led to the direct establishment of a genuinely democratic system. Even in the example of the American revolution, the political system that subsequently emerged was the result of deliberate political engineering by the framers of the American constitution rather than a natural corollary of the revolutionary experience. The dynamics involved in the working establishment of a democratic system often include a widely accepted democratic political culture, concerted efforts aimed at making democracy work and ensuring its survival, and a fundamental shift of priorities away from the attainment of specific national and economic goals and objectives into adherence to democratic rules and procedures.[11] These are not priorities that are high on the list of most revolutionaries's agendas, paling in importance compared to the need of securing newly-won privileges, erecting new institutions, inculcating new values, and fending off counter-revolutionaries. The connection between revolution and democracy is at best a historical coincidence, the latter being possible only long after the former has had time to settle and become part of the established political routine.

The wave of revolutions in east and central Europe in the late 1980s and early 1990s behind what used to be called the "Iron Curtain" has resulted in the manifestation of another axiom in the evolution of post-revolutionary systems, one generally absent from other historical cases. In one way or another, and with varying rates, all of the region's former communist governments have been overthrown and replaced by ostensibly democratic systems. Although the post-communist "democratic" regimes of

Poland, Hungary, Czechoslovakia, and the successor states to the former Soviet Union (Russia, Ukraine, Lithuania, Latvia, and Estonia) leave a great deal to be desired, a semblance of systematically-adopted democratic structures and procedures are beginning to emerge, or have already developed a rather firm footing.[12] The question then arises: why have these revolutions resulted in systems that are at least ostensibly democratic whereas in other past historical examples revolutions did not necessarily brought on such democracies?

The answer lies in the unique nature of the seemingly revolutionary events of the late 1980s. To begin with, it is not exactly clear whether the developments that at the time transpired in the region were essentially "negotiated" transfers of power or classic revolutions in the sense outlined here earlier. Even in the more archaic cases where events assumed a dynamic of their own, rather than being worked out through negotiations between departing communists and incoming elites, as was more or less the case in Poland and Czechoslovakia, the ominous threat of violent backlashes by communist regimes or their armed forces made extensive and careful negotiations between the two sides necessary. Detailed arrangements were carefully worked out whereby existing communist institutions would be replaced by those specifically designed to be democratic. Negotiations with the old elite took place simultaneous with elaborate and purposeful political engineering. Thus, the degree of spontaneity that characterize other revolutions and the workings of their internal, unfettered dynamics were in these instances unnaturally altered in order to deliberately control the course of ensuing events. The outcomes of such deliberate maneuvers might indeed be revolutionary compared to the character of the Old Orders that they replaced. However, as historical processes, one would be hard pressed to characterize these political transformations in central and eastern Europe in the same category as those of other classic revolutions.

Another element to consider in examining the outcomes of Europe's engineered revolutions is that of international forces. Europe's recent revolutions embodied two specific international features that were conspicuously absent from other revolutions. Firstly, these revolutions were occurring in an international environment and, more specifically, in a region in which democracy had by the 1980s become an established and sought-after norm. Regardless of their specific ideologies, post-revolutionary institutions in France in the 1790s, Russia in the 1920s and '30s, China in the 1950s, and Iran in the 1980s--as well as many other similar examples--did not evolve in regions where democratic principles and practices had ben firmly grounded. By the 1980s, however, most if not all of Europe had had a long and relatively successful marriage with democracy which the new-comers, who were escaping from the communist antithesis, could not overlook. If for no other reason, the element of a common cultural identity, jealously guarded by most Europeans, was an important determinant of the democratic character of Europe's post-communist regimes. Secondly, there is the even more important factor of economic needs. In each of the former communist countries of Europe, moves toward the establishment of democratic institutions were seen as instrumental in attracting economic assistance from abroad either in terms of direct grants or through investments. Whereas the foreign policies of other post-revolutionary states were inherently xenophobic or at least critical of the international status quo, the post-communist regimes of Europe have pursued policies aimed at international economic integration and acceptance by Europe's older--and rich-er--democracies. These are, after all, regimes that emerged after having lost the Cold War and are now eager to join the community of the victors. The other historical examples, however, all came about within and in turn waged both rhetorical and military wars of their own.

Whether the engineered, democratic revolutions of east and central Europe are historical aberrations or models for future revolutions to come remains to be seen. What is certain is that revolutions, in various shapes or forms, continue to remain distinct political and historic possibilities. Although revolutions occur with remarkable historical rarity, the circumstances which bring them about lurk beneath the surface in numerous Third World countries. Regimes that are narrowly-based, neopatrimonial, rely on unevolved and stunted institutions, and are inherently weak govern in many Third World nations over societies where frustrations and grievances are ready to erupt into mass violence. Despite moves toward democratization and more evolved and developed political systems in some Third World nations, particularly in Latin America and east Asia, there are still occasional flares of revolutionary fervor across the globe, even in the emerging democracies. Yet full-blown revolutions are infrequent, their occurrence depending on a coalescence of historical, political, socio-cultural, and international developments. So long as these developments do not simultaneously occur and manifest in specific revolutionary circumstances, instances of sporadic violence and instability are the most that these regimes face. Hope for revolutions, even if aborted, will continue to aspire generations of political activists in the Third World, so long as viable democratic systems remain largely alien to the region's political landscape. Only fully functioning democratic systems with socio-cultural and psychological resonance can fully safeguard against revolutions. Otherwise, in the many instances where normative means of political competition are absent, the tendency toward violence and revolutions remain an endemic probability. Whether the new wave of emerging democracies in the Third World prove capable of stemming the tide of engendered instability remains to be seen. What is certain is the enduring likelihood of further revolutionary eruptions in narrowly-based, delegitimized regimes promoting rapid social change and industrial development in the face of non-responsive and unchangeable political structures.

Notes

1. William Blanchard, *Revolutionary Morality: A Psychosexual Analysis of Twelve Revolutionists* (Oxford: Clio Press, 1984), p. xv.

2. Vernon Ruttan, "What Happened to Political Development?" *Economic Development and Cultural Change* vol. 32, no. 2 (January 1991), p. 279. Ruttan goes on to say that political development is also possible if "the distribution of power has become more equal, with no decline to the amount of power available to society."

3. Leonard Binder, "The Crises of Political Development," Leonard Binder, et al., *Crises and Sequences in Political Development* (Princeton, NJ: Princeton University Press, 1971), p. 68.

4. James Coleman, "The Development Syndrome: Differentiation Equality Capacity," Leonard Binder, et al., *Crises and Sequences in Political Development*, p. 75. Coleman argues that political developmet as represented in an "enhanced political capacity" is "consciously sought." In instances involving revolutions, however, political

development is a corollary of the revolutionary process *not* the willful efforts of the actors involved.

5. Ibid, p. 77.

6. Stephen Chilton, *Defining Political Development* (Boulder, CO: Lynne Rienner, 1988), p. 14.

7. Ibid, p. 28. For a "philosophical framework" to this definition of political development see Stephen Chilton, *Grounding Political Development* (Boulder, CO: Lynne Rienner, 1991).

8. Stephen Chilton, *Defining Political Development*, p. 80.

9. Ibid.

10. Ibid, p. 10.

11. A number of impressive works have in recent years examined the underlying dynamics involved in the process of democratization in selected Third World nations. See, for example, James Malloy and Mitchell Seligson, eds., *Authoritarians and Democrats: Regime Change in Latin America* (Pittsburgh: University of Pittsburgh Press, 1987); Guillermo O'Donnell, Phillipe Schmitter, and Lawrence Whitehead, eds., *Transitions from Authoritarian Rule: Comparative Perspective* (Baltimore: Johns Hopkins University Press, 1986); Louis Roniger, "Democratic Transition and Consolidation in Contemporary Southern Europe and Latin America," *International Journal of Comparative Sociology* vol. 30, nos. 3-4 (1989), pp. 216-29; Robert Fishman, "Rethinking State and Regime: Southern Europe's Transition to Democracy," *World Politics* vol. 42, no. 3 (April 1990), pp. 422-40.

12. As of this writing, Yugoslavia and Georgia are embroiled in bloody civil wars, and moves toward democracy by the post-communist governments of Albania, Romania, and Bulgaria have so far been halting at best. For an account of the revolutions of 1989 in Eastern Europe and their aftermaths see, Daniel Chirot, ed., *The Crisis of Leninism and the Decline of the Left: The Revolutions of 1989* (Seattle: University of Washington Press, 1991), especially Chap. 1.

Bibliography

Adelman, Irma and Jairus M. Hihn. "Crisis Politics in Developing Countries." *Economic Development and Cultural Change* vol. 33, no. 1 (October 1984): 1-22.

Adelman, Jonathan. *Revolution, Armies, and War: A Political History.* Boulder, CO: Lynne Rienner, 1985.

Aguirre, B.E. "The Conventionalization of Collective Behavior in Cuba." *American Journal of Sociology* vol. 90, no. 3 (1984): 541-66.

Al-Khalil, Samir. *Republic of Fear: The Politics of Modern Iraq.* Berkeley, CA: University of California Press, 1989.

Almond, Gabriel and Sidney Verba. *The Civic Culture.* London: Sage, 1989.

Almond, Gabriel and G. Bingham Powell. *Comparative Politics: System, Process, and Policy.* Houston: Little, Brown, 1978.

Alter, Peter. *Nationalism.* London: Routledge, 1989.

Anderson, Lisa. "Lawless Government and Illegal Opposition: Reflections on the Middle East." *Journal of International Affairs* vol. 42, no. 2 (Winter/Spring 1987): 219-232.

Andrain, Charles. *Political Change in the Third World.* Winchester, MA: Unwin Hyman, 1988.

Aya, Rod. "Theories of Revolution: Contrasting Models of Collective Violence." *Theory and Society* vol 8, no. 1 (July 1979): 39-99.

Badie, Bertrand and Pierre Birnbaum. *The Sociology of the State.* Arthur Goldhammer, trans. Chicago: University of Chicago Press, 1983.

Bakhash, Shaul. *The Reign of the Ayatollahs: Iran and the*

Islamic Republic. London: I.B. Tauris, 1985.

Beck, Carl. "Patterns and Problems of Governance". Carmelo Mesa-Lago and Carl Beck, eds. *Comparative Socialist Systems: Essays on Politics and Economy.* Pittsburgh: University Center for International Studies, 1975, 123-46.

Bigo, Pierre. *The Church and Third World Revolution.* Jeanne Marie Lyons, trans. New York: Orbis Books, 1977.

Binder, Leonard. "The Crisis of Political Development." Leonard Binder, et al. *Crisis and Sequences in Political Development.* Princeton, NJ: Princeton University Press, 1971: 3-72.

Blaufarb, D. and G. K. Tanham. *Who Will Win: A Key to the Puzzle of Revolutionary War.* London: Crane Russak & Co., 1989.

Blanchard, William. *Revolutionary Morality: A Psychosexual Analysis of Twelve Resolutionists.* Oxford: Clio Press, 1984.

Bloom, William. *Personal Identity, National Identity and International Relations.* Cambridge: Cambridge University Press, 1990.

Bosell, Terry and William Dixon. "Dependency and Rebellion: A Cross National Analysis." *American Sociological Review* vol. 55 (August 1990): 540-59.

Bozorgmehr, Mehdi and Georges Sabagh. "High Status Immigrants: A Statistical Profile of Iranians in the United States." *Iranian Studies* vol. 21, nos. 3-4 (1988): 5-35.

Breuilly, John. *Nationalism and the State.* New York: St. Martin's, 1982.

Brinton, Crane. *The Anatomy of Revolution.* New York: Prentice-Hall, 1952.

Bruneau, Thomas and Alex Macleod. *Politics in Contemporary Portugal: Parties and the Consolidation of Democracy.* Boulder, CO: Lynne Rienner, 1986.

Bruszt, Laszlo. "1989: The Negotiated Revolution in Hungary." *Social Research* vol. 57, no. 2 (Summer 1990): 365-87.

Calvert, Peter. *Politics, Power, and Revolution: An Introduction to Comparative Politics.* London: Wheatsheaf, 1983.

Caporaso, James, ed. *The Elusive State: International and Comparative Perspectives.* London: Sage, 1989.

Chaliand, Gerard. *Revolution in the Third World: Myths and Prospects.* New York: Viking Press, 1977.

Charques, Richard. *The Twilight of the Russian Empire*. Oxford: Oxford University Press, 1965, 204.

Chazan, Naomi, Robert Mortimer, John Ravenhill, and Donald Rothchild. *Politics and Society in Contemporary Africa*. Boulder, CO: Lynne Rienner, 1988.

Chilton, Stephen. "Defining Political Culture." *Western Political Quarterly* vol. 41, no. 3 (September 1988): 419-45.

_____. *Defining Political Development*. Boulder, CO: Lynne Rienner, 1988.

_____. *Grounding Political Development*. Boulder, CO: Lynne Rienner, 1991.

Chirot, Daniel, ed. *The Crisis of Leninism and the Decline of the Left: The Revolutions of 1989*. Seattle: University of Washington Press, 1991.

Claessen, Henry. "Changing Legitimacy." Ronald Cohen and Judith Toland, eds. *State Formation and Political Legitimacy*. New Brunswick, NJ: Transaction, 1988: 23-44.

Clapham, Christopher and George Philip, eds. *The Political Dilemmas of Military Regimes*. London: Rowman & Littlefield, 1985.

Colburn, Forrest. *Post-Revolutionary Nicaragua: State, Class, and the Dilemmas of Agrarian Policy*. Berkeley, CA: University of California Press, 1986.

Coleman, David and Frederick Nixson. *Economics of Change in Less Developed Countries*. London: Rowman & Littlefield, 1986.

Coleman, James S. "The Development Syndrome: Differentiation-Equality-Capacity." Leonard Binder, et al. *Crisis and Sequences in Political Development*. Princeton, NJ: Princeton University Press, 1971: 73-100

Conway, M. Margaret. "The Political Context of Political Behavior." *Journal of Politics*. vol. 15, no. 1 (February 1989), pp. 3-10.

Dalton, Russell J. "Generational Change in Elite Political Beliefs: The Growth of Ideological Polarization." *Journal of Politics* vol. 49 (October 1987): 976-97.

Daniels, Robert. "Russian Political Culture and the Post-Revolutionary Impasse." *The Russian Review* vol. 46 (1987): 165-76.

Davies, James. "Toward a Theory of Revolution." *American*

Sociological Review vol. 27, no. 1 (February 1962): 7-19.

_____. "Maslow and the Theory of Political Development: Getting to Fundamentals." *Political Psychology* vol. 12, no. 3 (1991): 389-420.

Davis, Harold E. *Revolutionaries, Traditionalists, and Dictators in Latin America.* London: Rowland & Littlefield, 1973.

Davis, John. *Libyan Politics: Tribe and Revolution.* California: 1988.

Decalo, Samuel. "Modalities of Civil-Military Stability in Africa." *The Journal of Modern African Studies* vol. 27, no. 4 (1989): 547-78.

DeFronzo, James. *Revolutions and Revolutionary Movements.* Boulder, CO: Westview Press, 1991.

Denyer, Tom. "The Ethics of Struggle." *Political Theory* vol. 17, no. 4 (November 1989): 535-49.

deSoto, Hernando. *The Other Path: The Invisible Revolution in the Third World.* London: I.B. Tauris, 1989.

DiPalma, Giuseppe. *To Craft Democracies: An Essay on Democratic Transitions.* Berkeley, CA: University of California Press, 1991.

Dittmer, Lowell. "Mao and the Politics of Revolutionary Morality." *Asian Survey* vol. XXVII, no. 3 (March 1987): 316-39.

Dix, Robert. 'The Varieties of Revolution." *Comparative Politics* vol. 15, no. 3 (April 1983): 281-94.

Dunn, John. *Modern Revolutions: An Introduction to the Analysis of a Political Phenomenon.* 2nd ed. Cambridge: Cambridge University Press, 1989.

_____. "Revolution." Terence Ball, James Farr, and Russel Hanson, eds. *Political Innovation and Conceptual Change.* Cambridge: Cambridge University Press, 1988.

_____. *Rethinking Modern Political Theory.* Cambridge: Cambridge University Press, 1985.

Eckhardt, William. "Authoritarianism." *Political Psychology* vol. 12, no. 1 (1991): 97-124.

Eckstein, Harry. "A Culturalist Theory of Political Change." *American Political Science Review* vol. 82, no. 3 (September 1988): 789-804.

Eisenstadt, S. N. *Revolution and the Transformation of Societies.* New York: Free Press, 1978.

Epstein, Edward. "Legitimacy, Institutionalization, and Opposition in Exclusive Bureaucratic Authoritarian Regimes: The Situation in the 1980s." *Comparative Politics* vol. 17, no. 1 (October 1984): 37-54.

Farhi, Farideh. "State Disintegration and Urban-Based Revolutionary Crisis: A Comparative Analysis of Iran and Nicaragua." *Comparative Political Studies* vol. 21, no. 2 (July 1988): 231-56.

Farr, James. "Historical Concepts in Political Science: The Case of Revolution." *American Journal of Political Science* vol. 26, no. 4 (November 1982) pp. 688-708.

Fishman, Robert. "Rethinking State and Regime: Southern Europe's Transition to Democracy." *World Politics* vol. 42, no. 4 (April 1990): 422-40.

Fleet, Michael. *The Rise and Fall of Chilean Christian Democracy.* Princeton, NJ: Princetin University Press, 1985.

Foltz, William. "External Causes." Barry Schutz and Robert Slater, eds. *Revolution and Political Change in the Third World.* Boulder, CO: Lynne Rienner, 1990: 54-68.

Freeman, Michael. "Review Article: Theories of Revolution." *British Journal of Political Science* vol. 2: 339-59.

Gamson, William. "Commitment and Agency in Social Movement." *Sociological Forum* vol. 6, no. 1 (1991): 27-50.

Gellner, Ernest. *Plough, Sword and Book: the Structure of Human History.* Chicago: University of Chicago Press, 1988.

Giddens, Anthony. *The Nation-State and Violence.* Berkeley, CA: University of California Press, 1985.

Gill, Graeme. *The Origins of the Stalinist Political System.* Cambridge: Cambridge University Press, 1990.

Goldstone, Jack. *Revolution and Rebellion in the Early Modern World.* Berkeley, CA: University of California Press, 1991.

———. "State Breakdown in the English Revolution: A New Synthesis." *American Journal of Sociology* vol. 92, no. 2 (September 1986): 257-322.

Goodwin, Jeff and Theda Skocpol. "Explaining Revolutions in the Contemporary World." *Politics and Society* vol. 17, no. 4 (December 1989): 489-509.

Gordon, David. *Images of the West: Third World Perspectives.* Savage, MD: Rowman & Littlefield, 1989.

Greenberg, Edward and Thomas Mayer. *Changes in the State:*

Causes and Consequences. London: Sage, 1990.

Green, Jerrold. "Counter Mobilization as a Revolutionary Form." *Comparative Politics* vol. 16, no. 2 (January 1984): 153-169.

Greene, Thomas. *Comparative Revolutionary Movements*. Englewood Cliffs, NJ: Prentice Hall, 1974.

Griffiths, John. "The Cuban Communist Party." Vicky Randall, ed. *Political Parties in the Third World*. London: Sage, 1988, 153-73.

Gugler, Josef. "The Urban Character of Contemporary Revolutions." Josef Gugler, ed. *The Urbanization of the Third World*. Oxford: Oxford University Press, 1988.

Gurr, Ted Robert. "War, Revolution, and the Growth of the Coercive State." *Comparative Political Studies* vol. 21, no. 1 (April 1988): 45-65.

_____. *Why Men Rebel?* Princeton, NJ: Princeton University Press, 1970.

Haferkamp, Hans and Neil Smelser, eds. *Social Change and Modernity*. Berkeley, CA: University of California Press: 1990.

Harris, Nigel. *City, Class and Trade: Social and Economic Change in the Third World*. London: I.B. Tauris, 1990.

_____. *National Liberation*. London: I.B. Tauris, 1990.

Held, David. *Political Theory and the Modern State: Essays on State, Power, and Democracy*. Stanford, CA: Stanford University Press, 1989.

Hermassi, Elbaki. *The Third World Reassessed*. Berkeley, CA: University of California, 1990.

Hernandez, Rafael and Harolda Dilla. "Political Culture and Popular Participation in Cuba." *Latin American Perspectives* issue 69, vol. 18, no. 2 (Spring 1991): 38-54.

Himmelstein, Jerome and Michael Kimmel. "Review Essay: The Implications and Limits of Skopol's Structure Model." *American Journal of Sociology* vol. 86, no. 5 (March 1981): 1145-54.

Hinnebusch, Raymond. "Charisma, Revolution, and State Formation: Qaddafi and Libya." *Third World Quarterly* vol. 7, no. 1 (January 1984): 59-73.

Hobsbawm, E. J. *Nations and Nationalism*. Cambridge: Cambridge University Press, 1990.

Hoffman, Stanley. "The Case for Leadership." *Foreign Policy* no.

81 (Winter 1990-1): 20-39.

Hong, Yung Lee. *From Revolutionary Cadres to Party Technocrats in Socialist China.* Berkeley, CA: University of California Press, 1990.

Horowitz, Dan. "Dual Authority Polities." *Comparative Politics* vol. 14, no. 3 (April 1982): 329-49.

Horowitz, Donald. *Coup Theories and Officers' Motives: Sri Lanka in Comparative Perspective.* Princeton, NJ: 1980.

Hourani, Albert. *The Emergence of the New Modern Middle East.* Berkeley, CA: University of California, 1981.

Hsu, Immanuel. *The Rise of Modern China.* 4th ed. Oxford: Oxford University Press, 1991.

Huntington, Samuel. "Social and Institutional Dynamics of One-Party Systems." Samuel Huntington, and Clement Moore, eds. *Authoritarian Politics in Modern Society.* London: Basic Books, 1970.

_____. *Political Order in Changing Societies.* New Haven, CT: Yale University Press, 1968.

Im, Hyug Baeg. "The Rise of Bureaucratic Authoritarianism in South Korea." *World Politics* vol. XXXIX, no. 2 (January 1987): 231-57.

Inglehart, Ronald. "The Renaissance of Political Culture." *American Political Science Review* vol. 82, no. 4 (December 1988): 1203-30.

Jackson, Robert. *Quasi-States: Sovereignty, International Relations, and the Third World.* Cambridge: Cambridge University Press, 1990.

Johnson, Chalmers. *Revolutionary Change.* London: Longman, 1983.

Jones, R. Ben. *The French Revolution.* London: Hodder & Stoughton, 1967.

Jowett, Garth and Victoria O'Donnel. *Propaganda and Persuasion.* London: Sage, 1986.

Kamrava, Mehran. "Causes and Leaders of Revolutions." *The Journal of Social, Political, and Economic Studies* vol. 15, no. 1 (Spring 1990): 79-89.

_____. *Revolution in Iran: Roots of Turmoil.* London: Routledge, 1990.

_____. *The Political History of Modern Iran: From Tribalism to Theocracy.* New York: Praeger, 1992.

_____. *Politics and Society in the Third World.* London: Routledge, 1993.

Kavanagh, Dennis. *Political Culture.* London: McMillan, 1972.

Keller, Edmond. *Revolutionary Ethiopia: From Empire to People's Republic.* Bloomington, IN: Indiana University Press, 1989.

_____. "Revolution and the Collapse of Traditional Monarchies: Ethiopia." Barry Schutz and Robert Slater, eds. *Revolution and Political Change in the Third World.* Boulder, CO: Lynne Rienner, 1990: 81-98.

Khoury, Philip and Joseph Costiner, eds. *Tribes and State Formation in the Middle East.* London: I.B. Tauris, 1991.

King, Roger. *The State in Modern Society: New Directions in Political Sociology.* Chatham, NJ: Chatham House, 1987.

Kowalewski, David. "Periphery Revolutions in World-System Perspective, 1821-1985." *Comparative Political Studies* vol. 24, no. 1 (April 1991): 76-99.

Krauss, Clifford. "Revolution in Central America?" *Foreign Affairs* vol. 65, no. 3 (1987): 564-581.

Kromnick, Isaac. "Reflections on Revolution: Definition and Explanation in Recent Scholarship." *History and Recent Theory* vol. XI, no. 1 (1972): 22-63.

Lancaster, Roger. *Thanks to God and the Revolution: Popular Religious and Class Consciousness in the New Nicaragua.* New York: Columbia University Press, 1988.

Leighley, Jan. "Participation as a Stimulus for Political Conceptualization." *The Journal of Politics* vol. 53, no. 1 (February 1991): 198-212.

LeoGrande, William. "Central America." Barry Schutz and Robert Slater, eds. *Revolution and Political Change in the Third World.* Boulder, CO: Lynne Rienner, 1990: 142-160.

Linz, Juan and Alfred Stepan, eds. *The Breakdown of Democratic Regimes.* Baltimore: Johns Hopkins University Press, 1978.

Lowder, Stella. *The Geography of Third World Cities.* London: Rowman & Littlefield, 1986.

McLennan, G.D. Held, S. Hall. *The Idea of the Modern State.* London: Open University Press, 1984.

McCormick, Gordon. "The Shining Path and Peruvian Terrorism." *The Journal of Strategic Studies* vol. 10, no. 4 (December

1987): 109-128.

Malloy, James and Mitchell Seligson, eds. *Authoritarians and Democrats: Regime Change in Latin America.* Pittsburgh: University of Pittsburgh Press, 1987.

Maravall, J. M. "Subjective Conditions and Revolutionary Conflicts: Some Remarks." *British Journal of Sociology* vol. 27, no. 1 (March 1976): 21-34.

Mason, T. David. "Indigenous Factors." Barry Schutz and Robert Slater, eds.*Revolution and Political Change in the Third World.* Boulder, CO: Lynne Rienner, 1990, 30-53.

Midlarsky, Manus. "Rulers and the Ruled: Patterned Inequality and the Onset of Mass Political Violence." *American Political Science Review* vol. 82, no. 2 (June 1988): 491-509.

_____. "Scarcity and Inequality: Prologue to the Onset of Mass Revolution." *Journal of Conflict Resolution* vol. 26, no. 1 (March 1982): 3-38.

Migdal, Joe. *Peasants, Politics, and Revolution: Pressures Toward Political and Social Change in the Third World.* Princeton, NJ: Princeton University Press, 1974.

Miroff, Bruce. *Pragmatic Illusions: The Presidential Politics of John F. Kennedy.* New York: David McKay, 1976.

Moghadam, Val. "Industrial Development, Culture and Working-Class Politics: A Case Study of Tabriz Industrial Workers in the Iranian Revolution." *International Sociology* vol. 2, no. 2 (June 1987): 151-175

Moore, Clement. "The Single Party as Source of Legitimacy." Samuel Huntington and Clement Moore, eds. *Authoritarian Politics in Modern Society.* London: Basic Books, 1970: 48-72.

Moore, Will. "Rebel Music: Appeals to Rebellion in Zimbabwe."*Political Communication* vol. 8, no. 2 (April-June 1991): 125-38.

Morley, Morris. *Imperial State and Revolutions: The United States and Cuba, 1952-1986.* Cambridge: Cambridge University Press, 1988.

O'Donnell, Guillermo, Philippe Schmitter, and Laurence Whitehead, eds.*Transitions from Authoritarian Rule: Prospects for Democracy.* Baltimore: Johns Hopkins University Press, 1985.

Ortega, Marvin. "The State, the Peasantry and the Sandanista Revolution." *Journal of Development Studies* vol. 26, no. 4

(1990):   122-42.

Ozbudun, Ergun. *Social Change and Political Participation in Turkey.* Princeton, NJ: Princeton University Press, 1976.

Paige, Jefferey. *Agrarian Revolution: Social Movements and Export Agriculture in the Underdeveloped World.* New York: Free Press, 1975.

Parsa, Misagh. "Theories of Collective Action and the Iranian Revolution." *Sociological Forum* vol. 3, no. 1 (Winter 1988): 41-71.

Paterson, Thomas, J.G. Clifford, and Kenneth Hegan. *American Foreign Policy: A History.* Lexington, MA: D.C. Heath & Co, 1991.

Portis, E.B. "Charismatic Leadership and Cultural Democracy." *Review of Politics* vol. 41, no 2 (February1987): 231-50.

Power, Timothy. "Political Landscapes, Political Parties, and Authoritarianism in Brazil and Chile." *International Journal of Comparative Sociology* vols. 29-30: 250-63.

Pye, Lucian. "The Legitimacy Crisis." Leonard Binder, et al. *Crisis and Sequence in Political Development.* Princeton, NJ: Princeton University Press, 1971: 135-158.

_____. "Identity and the Political Culture." Leonard Binder et al. *Crisis and Sequences in Political Development.* Princeton, NJ: Princeton University Press, 1971: 101-134.

_____. "Tiananmen and Chinese Political Culture." *Asian Survey* vol. 30, no. 4 (April 1990): 331-47.

Randall, Vicky. *Political Parties in the Third World.* London: Sage, 1988.

_____. "Introduction." Vicky Randall, ed. *Political Parties in the Third World.* London: Sage, 1988: 1-6.

Randall, Vicky and Robin Theobald. *Political Change and Underdevelopment: A Critical Introduction to Third World Politics.* London: McMillan, 1985.

Reardon, Kathleen. *Persuasion in Practice.* London: Sage, 1991.

Reich, Walter. *Origins of Terrorism: Psychologies, Ideologies, Theologies, States of Mind.* Cambridge: Cambridge University Press, 1990.

Reiman, Michael. *The Birth of Stalinism: The USSR on the Eve of the 'Second Revolution.'* London: I.B. Tauris, 1989.

Remmer, Karen. *Military Rule in Latin America.* Winchester, MA: Unwin Hyman, 1989.

Rice, Edward. *Wars of the Third Kind: Conflict in Underdeveloped Countries.* Berkeley, CA: University of California Press: 1988.

Roberts, Hugh. *Revolution and Resistance: Algerian Politics and the Kabyle Question.* London: I.B. Tauris, 1990.

Roniger, Loius. "Democratic Transition and Consolidation in Contemporary Southern Europe and Latin America." *International Journal of Comparative Sociology* vol. 30, nos. 3-4 (1989): 216-29.

Rosenbaum, Walter. *Political Culture.* New York: Praeger, 1975.

Rothgeb Jr., John M. "The Effects of Foreign Investment Upon Political Protest and Violence in Underdeveloped Societies." *The Western Political Quarterly* vol. 44, no. 1 (March 1991): 9-39.

Rouquie, Alain. *The Military and the State in Latin America.* Paul Sigmund, trans. Berkeley, CA: University of California Press, 1987.

Rubenstein, Richard. *Alchemists of Revolution: Terrorism in the Modern World.* London: I.B. Tauris, 1989.

Rubin, Barry. *Modern Dictators: Third World Coup Makers, Strongmen, and Populist Tyrants.* New York: McGraw Hill, 1987.

Rule, James. *Theories of Civil Violence.* Berkeley, CA: University of California Press, 1988.

Ruttan, Vernon W. "What Happened to Political Development." *Economic Development and Cultural Change* vol. 39, no. 2 (January 1991): 265-92.

Ryan, Michael. *Politics and Culture: Working Hypotheses for a Post-Revolutionary Society.* Baltimore: Johns Hopkins University Press, 1989.

Salert, Barbara. *Revolutions and Revolutionaries.* New York: Elsevier, 1976.

Sarduy, Pedro Perez. "Culture and the Cuban Revolution." *The Black Scholar* vol. 20, nos. 5-6 (Winter 1989): 17-23.

Scheye, Eric. "Psychological Notes on Central Europe: 1989 and Beyond." *Political Psychology* vol. 12, no. 2 (1991): 331-334.

Schubert, James N. "Age and Active-Passive Leadership Style." *American Political Science Review* vol. 82, no. 3 (September 1988): 763-72.

Schultz, Barry and Robert Slater. "Patterns of Legitimacy and

Future Revolutions in the Third World." Barry Schutz and Robert Slater, eds. *Revolution and Political Change in the Third World*. Boulder, CO: Lynne Rienner, 1990: 247-50.

_____. "A Framework for Analysis." Barry Schutz and Robert Slater, eds. *Revolution and Political Change in the Third World*. Boulder, CO: Lynne Rienner, 1990: 3-18.

Scott, James. "Hegemony and the Peasantry." *Politics and Society* vol. 7, no. 3 (1977): 267-96.

_____. *Domination and the Art of Resistance: Hidden Transcripts*. New Haven, CT: Yale University Press, 1990.

Seale, Patrick. *Asad of Syria: The Struggle for the Middle East*. Berkeley, CA: University of California Press: 1989.

Shingles, Richard D. "Class, Status, and Support for Government Aid to Disadvantaged Groups." *Journal of Politics* vol. 51, no. 4 (November 1989): 933-62.

Skocpol, Theda. "Social Revolutions and Mass Military Mobilization." *World Politics* vol. XI (January 1988): 147-68.

_____. "Rentier State and Shi'a Islam in the Iranian Revolution." *Theory and Society* vol. 11, no. 3 (May 1982): 265-283.

_____. "What Makes Peasants Revolutionary?" *Comparative Politics* vol. 14, no. 3 (April 1982): 351-375.

_____. *States and Social Revolutions*. Cambridge: Cambridge University Press, 1979.

Smith, Anthony D. "The Suspension of Nationalism." *International Journal of Comparative Sociology* vol. XXXI, nos. 1-2 (1990): 1-2.

Staar, Richard., ed. *1991 Yearbook on International Communist Affairs: Parties and Revolutionary Movements*. Stanford, CA: Hoover Institution Press, 1991.

Stark, Frank M. "Theories of Contemporary State Formation in Africa: a Reassessment." *The Journal of Modern African Studies* vol. 24, no. 2 (1986):

Steinberger, Peter J. "Ruling: Guardians and Philosopher-kings." *American Political Science Review* vol. 83, no. 4 (December 1989): 335-47.

Steinberger, Peter. "Ruling: Guardians and Philosopher-Kings." *American Political Science Review* vol. 83, no. 4 (December 1989): 1207-25.

Stepan, Alfred. *Democratizing Brazil: Problems of Transition and Consolidation.* Oxford: Oxford University Press, 1989.

Stone, L. "Theories of Revolution." *World Politics* vol 18 (1966): 159-76.

Teiwes, Fredrick. *Politics at Mao's Court: Gao Gang and Party Factionalism in the Early 1950s.* Armonk, NY: M.E. Sharp, 1990.

Vilas, Carlos. "Popular Insurgency and Social Revolution in Central America." *Latin American Perspectives* Issue 56, vol. 15, no. 1 (Winter 1988): 55-77.

Wald, Kenneth D. and Michael B. Lupfer. "'Human Nature' in Mass Political Thought: What People Think about People and What People Think about Politics." *Social Science Quarterly* vol. 68, (March 1987): 19-29.

Wallach, H.G. Peter. "Political Leadership." *Journal of Politics* vol. 50, no. 4 (November 1988): 1090-95.

Weber, Max. *On Charisma and Institution Building.* Chicago: University of Chicago Press, 1968.

Weiner, Myron. "Political Participation: Crisis of the Political Process." Leanord Binder, et al. *Crisis and Sequence in Political Development.* Princeton, NJ: Princeton University Press, 1971: 159-204.

White, Lynn. *Policies of Chaos: The Organizational Causes of Violence in China's Cultural Revolution.* Princeton, NJ: Princeton University Press, 1989.

Wiarda, Howard. "Political Culture and the Attraction of Marxism-Leninism: National Inferiority Complexes as an Explanatory Factor." *World Affairs* vol. 151, no. 3 (Winter 1988-89):143-9.

Wickham-Crowley, Timothy. "A Quantitative Comparative Approach to Latin American Revolutions." *International Journal of Comparative Sociology* vol. 32, nos. 1-2 (1991): 82-109.

Williame, Jean-Claude. "Political Success in Zaire, or Back to Machiavelli." *The Journal of African Studies* vol. 26, no. 1 (1988): 37-49.

Willner, Ann Ruth and Dorothy Willner. "The Rise and Role of Charismatic Leaders." Harvy Kebschull, ed. *Politics in Transitional Societies.* New York, NY: Appleton-Century-Crofts, 1973: 227-36.

Wolf, Eric. *Peasant Wars of the Twentieth Century.* New York: Harper and Row, 1969.

Wolpin, Miles. "Sociopolitical Radicalism and Military Professionalism in the Third World." *Comparative Politics* vol. 15, no. 2 (January 1983): 203-221.

_____. *Militarism and Social Revolution in the Third World.* Savage, MD: Rowman & Littlefield, 1981.

Zagorin, Perez. "Theories of Revolution in Contemporary Historiography." *Political Science Quarterly* vol. LXXXVIII, no. 1 (March 1973): 23-52.

Index

About the Author

MEHRAN KAMRAVA holds a Ph.D. in Social and Political Sciences from King's College, Cambridge University and is currently assistant professor of international studies at Rhodes College. He is the author of *Revolution in Iran: The Roots of Turmoil, Politics and Society in the Third World* and *The Political History of Modern Iran: From Tribalism to Theocracy* (Praeger, 1992).